P9-CKU-082

The Definitive
WIT
of Winston
Churchill

edited by

Richard M. Langworth

PublicAffairs
New York

Text © 2009 by The Estate of Winston S. Churchill
Editorial arrangement and contribution
© 2009 Richard M. Langworth

Published in the United States by PublicAffairs™,
a member of the Perseus Books Group.
Published in the United Kingdom
by Random House Group Ltd.
All rights reserved.
Printed in the United States of America.

No part of this book may be reproduced in any manner
whatsoever without written permission except in the case of
brief quotations embodied in critical articles and reviews. For
information, address PublicAffairs, 250 West 57th
Street, Suite 1321, New York, NY 10107.

PublicAffairs books are available at special discounts
for bulk purchases in the U.S. by corporations, institutions,
and other organizations. For more information, please contact
the Special Markets Department at the Perseus Books Group,
2300 Chestnut Street, Suite 200, Philadelphia, PA 19103,
call (800) 810-4145, extension 5000, or e-mail
special.markets@perseusbooks.com.

Library of Congress Cataloging-in-Publication Data
LCCN: 2009935119
ISBN: 978-1-58648-790-4
First Edition

10 9 8 7 6 5 4 3 2 1

Contents

Foreword

The Definitive Wit of Winston Churchill takes 'wit' to mean the capacity to provoke amusement or admiration by verbal dexterity or by the ability to associate words and thoughts in an arresting fashion. Churchill possessed that talent to a remarkable degree. As one of his successors as prime minister, Lord Home, used to observe, there was nothing Churchill loved more than 'to ambush the unexpected word or phrase'.

The habit sprang partly from an innate facility in the use of language, partly from brooding upon his own experience. Certainly it did not reflect systematic reading of the classics, for the teaching of English at Harrow concentrated more heavily upon grammar and syntax than upon the glories of English literature. The young man made up some of the deficiency by creating what his later coadjutor Bill Deakin termed his own school or university; that is, by settling upon lists of important books that he wished to read and then having them sent out to India. (We witness the same process at work later when he began to paint. He had some intermittent guidance from experts, but in all essentials taught himself. 'I never had any lessons, you know,' he would say.)

This characteristic – an anxiety to learn, a willingness to light new fields of interest in the mind (his own phrase, though used in a different context) – is endearing. It even extended to music. Until he was 80 or more, he sang the music-hall songs or hymns of his youth and relished the performance of military bands. And then when at last he had opportunity and inclination to hear something of a different kind, he discovered a taste for Beethoven, Sibelius and Brahms.

With a prodigious memory he could master large tracts of Gibbon or Macaulay, and at the same time remain untouched by much that someone more conventionally educated would have been expected to know. He had not read many of the great novels and had neglected notable poets. He was after all a man of fierce physical energy and restlessness, with endless pressing concerns from early youth to old age. His knowledge of literature, as of many other subjects, remained patchy. What he did know he knew extremely well, thanks to that wonderful power of recall. A couple of weeks after his severe stroke in the summer of 1953, he recited to his doctor Lord Moran long extracts from a poem by Longfellow. Asked when he had last read it, Churchill replied, 'About fifty years ago.'

> 'You will know, or Watson has written in vain, that I hold a vast store of out-of-the-way knowledge, without scientific system, but very available for the needs of my work. My mind is like a crowded box-room with packets of all sorts stowed away therein – so many that I may well have but a vague perception of what was there.'

Thus said Sherlock Holmes. Churchill used to put the point more prosaically by saying that he could generally dip his bucket into the well and come up with something useful.

For most purposes, his system worked admirably. What could be more just than his impromptu description in 1936 of Neville Chamberlain as 'the packhorse in our great affairs', a phrase remembered from Shakespeare and produced appositely at a dinner in Birmingham, while Baldwin was still prime minister but Chamberlain was known to shoulder a good part of the burden? As it chanced, however, Chamberlain was a thorough-going expert in Shakespearean texts, which WSC was not. It thus amused the former, and perhaps mortified the latter a little, to realise that because he had not checked the quotation before speaking, he had attributed it to the wrong play.

We may take 'humour' to mean in this context a capacity to detect the funny or the ludicrous, the frivolous treatment of an apparently solemn subject, in particular the capacity to see a joke against oneself; there is something less refined or delicate about humour than about wit. If we must make a choice, WSC may be accounted more of a wit than a humorist.

This is a work that allows the reader to make the comparison, a book made possible by processes of scanning and storage which would have interested Churchill enormously; for his curiosity about science and its applications extended from floating harbours to his own ailments.

Few politicians have owed more than Churchill to command of language. Nor have the sayings and writings of any other modern statesman been so fully preserved. It has been the editor's lot in consequence to sift and winnow an enormous volume of material. Even so, we must realise with chagrin that many of Churchill's utterances are lost to us. Lady Violet Bonham Carter, for example, recorded after visiting WSC, 'As we went upstairs he reeled out a long magnificent sentence and said, "Now remember that. I shall never say it so well again"'; and against this entry, many years later, she noted, 'Alas, I have forgotten it!'

David Dilks
(formerly Vice-Chancellor of the University
of Hull; author of *The Great Dominion:
Winston Churchill in Canada 1900–1954*)

Introduction

Oh dear. I can see the reviews and weblogs now: 'Langworth says Churchill thought of Russians as "baboons" and Germans as "carnivorous sheep".' No, I do not say these things. In fact, Churchill admired Russians for valour and Germans for ingenuity, among other things.

So let us establish at the outset that *The Definitive Wit of Winston Churchill* is a *partial* collection of his best quotations – *limited to witticisms*. In the words of David Dilks, it is 'a bonsai version' of *Churchill by Himself* – my comprehensive collection of Churchill quotations from these same publishers – plus some 150 new entries chosen for their wit and humour.

The danger in culling witticisms from Churchill's 15 million published words is that they may suggest a warped view of his broader attitudes. Take for example Poland, in which the sole entry here, from many thousands of words on the subject, involves stuffing the 'Polish goose' with territory after World War II. This is not representative of Churchill's broad admiration for the Polish state or the valiant Poles who fought in World War II, or his friendships with men like Sikorski. In such cases I was tempted to add a majestic and inspiring quotation: 'The soul of Poland is indestructible ...' But I adhered to my mandate: witticisms alone. For readers who want more, *Churchill by Himself* contains over 4,000 quotations in 34 chapters, a comprehensive collection from the amusing to the sublime.

Churchill's words, and 35 million more words about him by colleagues, biographers and friends, are the digital database that informs this book. In 1997 Karl-Georg Schon, then a German university student, kindly sent me optical scans of most of Churchill's published works and of several hundred books about him. I have received key additional scanning assistance from

Wayne Brent, president of Zuma Corporation in Culver City, California, and his capable technical wizard, Alfredo Alvarez. My son Ian, a software engineer, later collected my digital treasure trove in a format enabling me to track any word or phrase (the vast majority from Churchill's own works) to its source. Virtually all quotations in this book are backed by verifiable sources; no item is included unless it can be attributed.

The usual order is alphabetical by subject, then chronological by date, though large subjects (like World War II) get a subsection (within the 'War' chapter). Quotations carrying a date only in the bibliographical notes are from Churchill's speeches in the House of Commons: the Parliamentary Debates (Hansard). All other quotes are specifically referenced with 'key words', which are identified in the bibliography. For example, 'Official Biography' refers to the official biography, *Winston S. Churchill*, by Randolph S. Churchill and Sir Martin Gilbert: its biographic and companion or document volumes (see Bibliography).

Dates cited are the earliest attributable to the quotations. I have sometimes indicated the date of a quotation *and* when it was later published, especially concerning the two World Wars. Venues other than London, Chartwell or Downing Street are supplied if available. Quotes from broadcasts are identified and sources noted.

Red herrings

The internet is an electronic Hyde Park Corner of words and opinions, and several Churchill quote books contain many inaccuracies. Scores of quotations that Churchill never said or that have been repeated from some prior source muddy the canon. The test of any quotation is whether it has reliable attribution. If there is none, it is probably a 'red herring'. The most common examples are in the Appendix.

Thanks

Professor David Dilks sent me comprehensive notes on *Churchill by Himself*, which helped me to detect many slips and fine points in that book for future printings and a posted guide on the internet. I immediately asked him to help me check this new book. Not only has he saved me from myself in scores of cases, but he has provided a goodly number of new witticisms from his own experience and writings, and a Foreword that really tells you what the book aims to do.

To the aforementioned Karl-Georg Schon, Wayne Brent, Alfredo Alvarez and Ian Langworth, along with my wife Barbara (with me every step of the way), my gratitude is enormous. I thank Winston S. Churchill for authorising the use of his grandfather's copyright, and Gordon Wise at Curtis Brown Ltd for finding the best publishers possible in Ebury Press and PublicAffairs. The people at Ebury Press, Andrew Goodfellow and Ali Nightingale; and Clive Priddle, Dan Ozzi and Niki Papadopoulos at Perseus Books and PublicAffairs, deserve an advance thanks, for most of my work is now done, and theirs is just beginning.

Several Churchill Centre members have helped and inspired entries, including Randy Barber, David Boler, Paul Courtenay, Laurence Geller, Chris Matthews, Marcus Frost, General Colin L. Powell, Ambassador Paul H. Robinson and Suzanne Sigman. Ralph Keyes, editor-author of *The Quote Verifier*, helped me to get into my bones the essence and language of a good book of quotations. Fred Shapiro, editor of *The Yale Book of Quotations*, also offered sound judgement and advice.

Many others deserve credit for their help, inspiration, research or material over the years. In alphabetical order they include but are not limited to Professor Paul Addison; William F. Buckley, Jr; Senator Harry F. Byrd, Jr; Professor Antoine Capet; Minnie Churchill; Peregrine Churchill; Winston Churchill; The Hon. Clark Clifford; Ronald I. Cohen; Sir John Colville; Michael Dobbs; Sir Martin Gilbert; Ronald Golding; Grace Hamblin; Glenn Horowitz; Professor Warren Kimball; James Lancaster; Sir Fitzroy Maclean; Professor James W. Muller; Edmund Murray; Elizabeth Nel; Oscar Nemon; The Hon. Celia Sandys; Christian Pol-Roger; Professor David Reynolds; Andrew Roberts; Arthur M. Schlesinger, Jr; Lord Soames; Professor David Stafford;

Haakon Waage; and Mark Weber. Lastly I thank Sir Winston Leonard Spencer Churchill, KG, OM, PC. Where would we all be without him?

I am most anxious to hear from readers who wish to offer comments, corrections, praise or blame, to which end I refer readers to the reviews section of my website, http://richardlangworth. com, where any follow-up notes will be published.

Richard M. Langworth
High Tide
Eleuthera
Bahamas
14 March 2009
dw-rml@sneakemail.com

1. Thrusts and parries

Churchill has a deserved reputation for lightning parries and razor-edged thrusts at critics and opponents. Anthony Eden was ready of speech and needed only a few notes to hold forth, which is why Churchill so often opened debates with a carefully prepared oration, and Eden closed them. Churchill's friend F. E. Smith (Lord Birkenhead) did utter some of the barbs often credited to WSC, but Churchill in quick retort had few equals.

Like Groucho Marx, Churchill had his straight men and sparring partners, particularly at Question Time in the House of Commons, which he relished and carefully anticipated. Two of these were the Labour MPs Emanuel Shinwell and Emrys Hughes, who in the 1950s held him in an odd affection which WSC returned. He gave less quarter to his most serious Labour foe, Aneurin Bevan, or to the sillier Conservatives, particularly the fussy and aptly named Sir Waldron Smithers.

Churchill would often lie in wait for the opportunity to loose a verbal ambuscade, which he had carefully composed and filed in his photographic memory. Still, he wasn't always able to rehearse the retort, and some of his ad libs during Question Time are as good as that honourable custom has produced.

Aborigine missionaries

Mr Hughes (Labour): Is the Prime Minister aware that the Australian aborigines who are converted to Christianity are now thinking of sending missionaries to this country, because they think that the atom bomb can only have been invented by savages and barbarians?

WSC: I hope that the Leader of the Opposition will not feel unduly hurt.

1952 *Under Attlee's premiership (1945–51) the British atomic bomb had been built and was made possible only because the annual Estimates to Parliament were deliberately falsified, year after year.*

Above comprehension

Mr Lewis (Labour): Is the Prime Minister aware of the deep concern felt by the people of this country at the whole question of the Korean conflict?

WSC: I am fully aware of the deep concern felt by the Hon. Member in many matters above his comprehension.

1952[1]

Mr M. Stewart (Labour): Will the Prime Minister remember the Greek proverb, 'Much learning does not teach sense'?

Mr Lewis (Labour): May I ask the Prime Minister whether that is above his comprehension?

WSC: I am sorry to see that I hit so deeply home.

1952[2]

Abstaining

WSC: We [Conservatives] thought it better and wiser to abstain as a body, and that is the course we intend to pursue.

Mr Bevin: How can you pursue it when you are sitting still?

WSC: We are discussing the movements of the mind, and not the much more bulky shiftings of the human body.

1945

Abuse

Mr Attlee (Labour): The Rt. Hon. Gentleman has often heard, 'No case, abuse the other side.'

WSC: With great respect, I would ask your permission, Mr Speaker, to correct the misquotation – 'When you have no case, abuse the plaintiff's attorney.'

1953 *WSC had announced the merging of two government departments. Labour doubted that this would save money.*

Agitated opponents

WSC: I was very much surprised that the Hon. Member for Silvertown [Jack Jones, MP], who certainly does not bear the reputation of being mealy-mouthed, should have been brought into such a state of extreme agitation by language which, I should have thought, a man of his moral fibre and physical structure could have afforded to sustain with a fair degree of composure.

1921

Alcohol

Mormon visitor, when offered a whisky and soda: May I have water, Sir Winston? Lions drink it.

WSC: Asses drink it too.

Second Mormon: Strong drink rageth and stingeth like a serpent.

WSC: I have long been looking for a drink like that.

1950s[1]

WSC: Prof., pray calculate the amount of champagne and spirits I have consumed in my life and indicate how much of this room they would fill.

Lindemann, pretending to calculate with his slide rule: I'm afraid not more than a few inches, Winston.

WSC: How much to do, how little time remains![2]

A favourite enquiry about WSC's alcohol intake, usually enacted with the help of 'the Prof.', his friend Professor Lindemann.

Anglo-American mongrel

Field Marshal Slim: I suppose we shall end up with some mongrel weapon, half British and half American.

WSC: Pray moderate your language, Field Marshal – that's an exact description of me.

1952 *Churchill as the new prime minister in 1951 inherited the controversy over the relative merits of the new British and American automatic rifles. Field Marshal Sir William Slim, Chief of the Imperial General Staff, voiced his opinion.*

Baskets in egg

Alan Lennox-Boyd: You don't want to have all your eggs in one basket.

WSC: On the contrary, I don't want all those baskets in one egg.

1953 or 1954 *Minister of Transport Lennox-Boyd proposed to fly a large number of Conservative MPs to a conference in Italy to demonstrate confidence in the redesigned Comet aircraft.*

Baths

Hugh Gaitskell (Labour): Personally, I have never had a great many baths myself, and I can assure those who are in the habit of having a great many that it does not make a great difference to their health if they have less.

WSC: When Ministers of the Crown speak like this on behalf of His Majesty's Government, the Prime Minister and his friends have no need to wonder why they are getting increasingly into bad odour. I had even asked myself, when meditating upon these points whether you, Mr Speaker, would admit the word 'lousy' as a parliamentary expression in referring to the administration, provided, of course, it was not intended in a contemptuous sense but purely as one of factual narration.

1947 *Gaitskell, Minister of Fuel and Power in the post-war Labour Government, was urging energy conservation; his advice proved too much for Churchill, a renowned bather.*

Bloody black sheep

Mr Maurice Webb: We are like a lot of sheep, aren't we?

WSC: Yes, bloody black sheep.

1946

Brighton

WSC: And what, pray, are you doing in Brighton?

Alan Lennox-Boyd: Oh, just taking a day or two's rest.

WSC: Nonsense! A man in the prime of life can have only one reason for being in Brighton in mid-week.

1952[1] *Lennox-Boyd had left London in secret for his wife's flat at the seaside. Churchill ferreted him out.*

WSC: Where are you going to, my dear?

Harold Macmillan: I am going to Brighton.

WSC: Oh! Racing, I suppose.

Macmillan: No, Prime Minister, I'm going to a meeting of accountants.

WSC: Turf accountants, I trust? That should be jolly.

circa 1953[2] *'Turf accountants' is racing parlance for bookmakers.*

Bring a friend

Bernard Shaw: Am reserving two tickets for you for my premiere. Come and bring a friend – if you have one.

WSC: Impossible to be present for the first performance. Will attend the second – if there is one.

1922 *The play was* Saint Joan. *It had a good run. Sometimes this is misdated as 1932.*

Combing out

The War Office was urging the 'combing out' of various industries or departments.

WSC: Physician, comb thyself.

1916

Constipation

WSC: Ah, there goes that constipated Britannia.

circa 1948 *Not as famous as the 'you are drunk … you are ugly' exchange (see Drunk and ugly below), this nevertheless is an accurate description of what Lord Carrington described as 'the portly Labour MP', Bessie Braddock.*

Crackling of thorns

WSC: ... our policy is an adequate basic standard – within just laws, let the best man win. [Laughter] The crackling of thorns under a pot does not deter me.

1947 *Churchill, defending Conservative Party policy, replied to Labour ridicule by recalling Ecclesiastes VII:6: 'For as the crackling of thorns under a pot, so is the laughter of the fool: this also is vanity.'*

Craft

WSC: [Labour will] make the British people drain their cup to the last dregs ... Here I see the hand of the master craftsman, the Lord President.

Herbert Morrison, Lord President: The Rt. Hon. Gentleman has promoted me.

WSC: Craft is common both to skill and deceit.

1947

Crooked deal

Mr Frederick Pethick-Lawrence: The Rt. Hon. Gentleman, like a bad bridge player, blames his cards.

WSC: I blame the crooked deal.

circa 1930

Damned old fool

Mr Snow (Labour): Damned old fool.

Colonel Gomme-Duncan (Conservative): Is it in order for an Hon. Member to refer to the Rt. Hon. Gentleman as 'a damned old fool'?

Mr Snow: I beg to withdraw that statement and to apologise but, of course, the Rt. Hon. Gentleman has been extremely provocative.

Hon. Members: Get out.

WSC: The Hon. Gentleman must accept the position of being subordinate; although let me make it quite clear that this is the first time that I have ever heard the word 'subordinate' regarded as unparliamentary or even as almost an obscene expression. However, the damned old fool has accepted the apology.

1951

de Gaulle, Charles

Brendan Bracken: But … remember, Winston … he thinks of himself as the reincarnation of Saint Joan.

WSC: Yes, but my bishops won't burn him!

1943[1]

de Gaulle: Finally I am your prisoner. Soon you will send me to the Isle of Man.

WSC: No. Since you are a distinguished general, I will send you to the Tower of London.

1943[2] *The actual exchange was in French. De Gaulle said: 'Bientôt vous m'enverrez à l'iloman.' Only at the third attempt did the interpreter elicit the fact that 'l'iloman' meant 'the Isle of Man'.*

Dead birds

Aneurin Bevan: Winston, for heaven's sake, your flies are undone.

WSC: You needn't bother yourself about that. Dead birds never fly from the nest.

circa 1946 *Bevan had arrived at the palace in a lounge suit. WSC, resplendent in court dress, had started the exchange by saying, 'Well! At least you could have come properly dressed.'*

Dead or alive

Michael Collins: You hunted me night and day. You put a price on my head.

WSC: Wait a minute. You are not the only one. At any rate it was a good price – £5,000. Look at me – £25 dead or alive. How would you like that?

1924 *The IRA's Michael Collins was in London to negotiate the Irish*

Treaty, which gave Home Rule to the South of Ireland and left Ulster in the Union. Collins, Churchill remarked, 'was in his most difficult mood, full of reproaches and defiances'. But after reading Churchill's wanted poster from the Boer War, Collins 'broke into a hearty laugh. All his irritation vanished ...'

Deaf member

WSC: Look at that fellow ignoring the advantages which a beneficent Providence has bestowed upon him.

undated *On seeing an elderly MP striving to catch a speech through an ear trumpet.*

Dirty dogs and palings

Sir William Paling (Labour, Dewsbury) violated parliamentary decorum by shouting at Churchill, 'Dirty dog!'

WSC: May I remind the Hon. Member for Dewsbury what dogs, dirty or otherwise, do to palings?

circa 1945–51

Discards

Sir J. E. Masterton-Smith: But, First Lord, you discarded the knave.

WSC: The cards I throw away are not worthy of observation or I should not discard them. It is the cards I play on which you should concentrate your attention.

1912 *During a bridge game on the Admiralty yacht* Enchantress, *when WSC was First Lord of the Admiralty.*

Doing what is right

Field Marshal Alexander: Well, Prime Minister, I am a soldier and don't know much about politics; but I think we should do whatever is decent, fair, right and honourable.

WSC: Never in my long experience have I heard so outrageous a doctrine propounded by a Minister of the Crown.

circa 1953

Driving on the left

Richard Miles, from the British Embassy in Washington, suggested Britain might contribute to Anglo-American understanding by switching to driving on the right.

WSC: No! No! It won't do. If a band of ruffians should set upon you, your sword arm wouldn't be free!

1942

Drunk and ugly

Bessie Braddock, MP: Winston, you are drunk, and what's more you are disgustingly drunk.

WSC: Bessie, my dear, you are ugly, and what's more, you are disgustingly ugly. But tomorrow I shall be sober and you will still be disgustingly ugly.

1946 *A world-famous exchange, and confirmed by a bodyguard present as WSC was leaving the House of Commons. Lady Soames, who knows her father was always gallant to ladies, doubted the story – but the bodyguard explained that WSC was not drunk, just tired and wobbly, which caused him to fire the full arsenal. WSC was probably relying on his photographic memory for this riposte: in the 1934 movie* It's a Gift, *W. C. Fields's character, when told he is drunk, responds, 'Yeah, and you're crazy. But I'll be sober tomorrow and you'll be crazy the rest of your life.'*

Facts

WSC: I like the martial and commanding air with which the Rt. Hon. Gentleman [George Wyndham, MP] treats facts. He stands no nonsense from them.

1909

Fair case

Cabinet minister after long discussion: I have tried to put the case fairly.

WSC: A very dangerous thing to do.

1950s

Feet on the ground

WSC: I am sorry if personal jealousies, or other motives below the level of events, have led the Socialist Party at first to embark upon the unnatural plan of narrowing United Europe down to United Socialist Europe ... I hope that their recent publication, 'Facing the Facts', or 'Face the Facts' ...

Hon. Members: 'Feet on the Ground'.

WSC: 'Feet on the Ground'. If Hon. Gentlemen opposite were to persist very long in facing the facts they would find their feet on the ground. And they might very soon find the rest of their bodies there as well.

1948

Food Ministry

Mr I. O. Thomas (Labour): Will the Prime Minister indicate if he will take the precaution of consulting the consuming public before he decides to abolish the Food Ministry?

WSC: On the whole, I have always found myself on the side of the consumer.

1953

Foot and mouth disease

Mr Boothby (Conservative, Aberdeen): Is my Rt. Hon. Friend aware that there is a torrent of complaints from Scotland at the present time?

WSC: I am sure my Hon. Friend would be fully capable of giving full vent to any such torrent, but the difficulty is that we are not sure that foot and mouth disease is as well educated on the subject of borders and questions arising out of them as he is.

Mr Boothby: I beg to give notice that I shall raise this matter on the adjournment.

WSC: I am afraid I cannot undertake to be present when this new red herring is drawn across the border.

1952 *Boothby wanted foot and mouth disease in Scotland to be handled in Edinburgh rather than by the Ministry of Agriculture in London.*

Force and favour

An MP in the division lobbies, as Churchill forged forward: It's wonderful to see Winston bulldozing his way through, in spite of his growing deafness and the noisy lobby.

WSC: Partly by force, partly by favour!

1955

Foreign secretaries unite

WSC: Foreign secretaries of the world unite; you have nothing to lose but your jobs.

1954 *A paraphrase of Marx's 'Workers of the world unite. You have nothing to lose but your chains.'*

Foresight

Mr Jay (Labour): Would we be right in inferring from the Prime Minister's answer that he himself has given no thought to this question?

WSC: That would be a rather hazardous assumption on the part of the Rt. Hon. Gentleman, who has not, so far as I am aware, at any time in his parliamentary career distinguished himself for foresight.

1952

Frustrated teacher

Harrow tutor Mr Mayo, circa 1888: I don't know what to do with you boys!

WSC: Teach us, sir!

1954

God and the House

Sir Stafford Cripps: I fear only God and the House of Commons.

WSC: I do hope God gets the better deal.

1940s

Guillotine

WSC: We have all heard of how Dr Guillotin was executed by the instrument that he invented.

Sir Herbert Samuel: He was not!

WSC: Well, he ought to have been.

1931

Guilty conscience

WSC: My Rt. Hon. Friend … has not been long enough in office to grow a guilty conscience.

1938 *WSC was referring to Sir Kingsley Wood, Air Minister from May 1938 to April 1940.*

Gut meets gut

WSC: But what happens when two guts meet – or gut meets gut, so to speak?

1949 *WSC asked who should command the Home Guard. Eden said he supposed it would be the man with the greatest guts.*

Hanging

WSC: Hanging, under English law, if properly conducted, is, I believe, an absolutely painless death.

Mr A. E. Stubbs: Try it.

WSC: Well, it may come to that.

1948[1] *Churchill was comparing life imprisonment with what he regarded as the preferable death sentence.*

A female admirer: Doesn't it thrill you … to know that every time you make a speech the hall is packed to overflowing?

WSC: It is quite flattering, but whenever I feel this way I always remember that if instead of making a political speech I was being hanged, the crowd would be twice as big.

1952[2]

Health

Photographer: I hope, sir, that I will shoot your picture on your hundredth birthday.

WSC: I don't see why not, young man. You look reasonably fit and healthy.

1949 *WSC was celebrating his seventy-fifth birthday.*

Impartial historian

WSC: ... it is absolutely necessary to invoke the great name of Mr Gladstone, a name which is received with reverence below the gangway on the opposition side, and with a certain amount of respect by some Hon. Members who sit opposite.

Hon. Members: What about yourself?

WSC: I occupy the impartial position of historian.

1927

Indians

Mrs Ogden Reid: What are you going to do about those wretched Indians?

WSC: Before we proceed further let us get one thing clear. Are we talking about the brown Indians in India, who have multiplied alarmingly under the benevolent British rule? Or are we speaking of the red Indians in America who, I understand, are almost extinct?

1943 *President Roosevelt mischievously invited to lunch the Vice-President and de facto publisher of the* New York Herald Tribune, *a notable campaigner for India's independence. Her query came on the White House verandah. Mrs Reid was rendered speechless, and Roosevelt was convulsed with laughter.*

Indignation

WSC: My Hon. and Gallant Friend [Captain Wedgwood Benn] must really not develop more indignation than he can sustain.

1920[1] *Wedgwood Benn had worked himself into what seemed to be apoplexy over a speech Churchill was making.*

WSC: Human beings, happily for them, do not have to direct all their bodily functions themselves … No official quota is set for lymph or bile. Otherwise I fear the President of the Board of Trade [Sir Stafford Cripps] would find he had overdrawn his account very much.

1945[2]

Ingratitude

WSC was told that a German bomb had fallen on former prime minister Stanley Baldwin's London house.

WSC: What base ingratitude!

1940

Jujube

WSC: I was only looking for a jujube!

1951 *During a speech by Hugh Gaitskell, WSC, on the opposition front bench, began searching his pockets, then the floor, derailing Gaitskell, who finally stopped speaking and offered to assist in the search. The* Scotsman *recorded the incident the next day as 'The Fall of the Pastille'.*

Korea vs Crimea

Mr Harold Davies (Labour): Does the Rt. Hon. Gentleman realise that the House is getting less information on the Korean situation than his equally great predecessor Mr Gladstone was giving the House in the time of the Crimean War?

WSC: I am afraid I have not at my fingers' ends the exact part which Mr Gladstone took in the Crimean War. It was even before my time.

1952

Korean armaments

Churchill was asked where the North Korean armaments had come from.

Sir Waldron Smithers (Conservative): Moscow.

WSC: Although there are movements ever being made in aerial locomotion, it would be premature to suppose that they came from the moon.

1952

Latin: 'O, table'

WSC: What does it mean, sir?

Form master: 'O, table' is the vocative case ... you would use that in addressing a table, in invoking a table.

WSC: But I never do!

1930 It was 1888. Winston's form master led him to an empty classroom and asked him to learn the first declension of mensa, *the Latin word for 'table'. The master returned and Churchill posed his question.*

Making up his mind

Emanuel Shinwell (Labour): Why can he not make up his mind?

WSC: I long ago made up my mind. The question is to get other people to agree.

1952

Marriage

Randolph, WSC's son, had just married Pamela Digby. Someone suggested to WSC that Randolph and his new bride did not have enough money to marry.

WSC: What do they need? Cigars, champagne and a double bed.

1939

Ministry of Economic Warfare

WSC: I only marked the paper 'M.E.W.' It seems he has mewed.

1940 Churchill had forwarded a paper suggesting that a Foreign Office proposal would be opposed by the Minister of Economic Warfare, who replied that he would do so.

Moustache and politics

Newly introduced young woman: There are two things I don't like about you – your new moustache and your new political party.

WSC: Pray do not disturb yourself, you are not likely to come into contact with either.

1900 *Since Churchill cultivated a moustache only briefly, during and after the Boer War, this had to be around the time of his first campaign for Parliament.*

Naked encounter

WSC: The prime minister of Great Britain has nothing to hide from the president of the United States.

Or: You see, Mr President, I have nothing to hide.

1941[1] *Uncertain but possible: Roosevelt, inspired to call the new world body 'United Nations', wheeled himself into Churchill's room, finding the PM, as Harry Hopkins said, 'stark naked and gleaming pink from his bath'. Later, queried by FDR biographer Robert Sherwood, WSC said: 'I could not possibly have made such a statement as that. The President himself would have been well aware that it was not strictly true.' Whatever was said, such an encounter apparently did happen: see next entry.*

WSC: Sir, I believe I am the only man in the world to have received the head of a nation naked.

1942[2] *WSC to the king, recounted by WSC to Roosevelt, then by FDR to his confidante Daisy Suckley and the British ambassador, Lord Halifax, on 17 January 1945. In this version, WSC did not say he had 'nothing to hide', which he denied to Robert Sherwood. FDR simply said, 'United Nations!' and Churchill responded, 'Good!'*

Nein demerits

Schoolmistress: Nine demerits seems even too much for you, Winston.

WSC: The word I used was *nein*, German for no.

1882 *At the end of a school day he lined up with other students to report their day's demerits.*

Old-age ailments

Tory member: They say the old man's getting a bit past it.

WSC: And they say that the old man's getting deaf as well.

1960 *Halle provides a second rejoinder (341): Lord Hinchingbrooke: He can't hear you, he's very deaf. WSC replied: Yes, and they say the old man is gaga too.*

Opinions

WSC: If I valued the Hon. Gentleman's [Sir J. Lonsdale, MP] opinion I might get angry.

1913

Patience in Parliament

WSC: The Hon. Member should not get so excited ... I was eleven years a fairly solitary figure in this House and pursued my way in patience and so there may be hope for the Hon. Member ...

1944 *Churchill was often interrupted by Willie Gallacher (1881–1965), the only Communist MP from 1935 to 1945, when another one was elected. I cannot verify a WSC reference to Gallacher as a Member 'who consents to be used as the pawn and utensil of a foreign power ... Shut up, Moscow!' (allegedly 1947 Halle 1966, 244) Gallacher is supposed to have responded: 'Shut up, voice of Wall Street.'*

Practice

WSC: I can well understand the Hon. Member speaking for practice, which he badly needs.

1920 *Response to a speech by Sir Oswald Mosley, who was known for his frequent and superfluous speeches.*

Prayer

Someone remarked that Greek archbishop Damaskinos was in the habit of securing himself from interruption by hanging a notice on his door: 'His Beatitude is at prayer.'

WSC: I'd like to try that at Downing Street, but I'm afraid no one would believe it.

1944 *Churchill installed Archbishop Damaskinos, whom he at first regarded as a 'scheming medieval prelate' and 'pestilent priest from the Middle Ages', as a regent in Greece to quell warring factions. He was soon impressed by Damaskinos, not least by the news that the archbishop in his youth had been a champion wrestler.*

President, running for

Reporter: Would you become an American citizen if we could make you president of the United States?

WSC: There are various little difficulties in the way. However, I have been treated so splendidly in the United States that I should be disposed, if you can amend the constitution, seriously to consider the matter.

1932

Prigs and prudes

Walter Runciman (WSC's 1899 Liberal opponent): I have not been a swashbuckler around the world.

WSC: And I do not belong to a radical party composed of prigs, prudes and faddists.

1899

Primus inter pares

WSC: As to the chairman of the committee, he is not *'facile princeps'*, but *'primus inter pares'* ...

Labour members rose at a perceived slur on their non-classical educations; some demanded, 'Translate!'

WSC: ... which, for the benefit of any old Etonians who may be present, I should, if very severely pressed, venture to translate.

1941 *When offering to translate, Churchill, an old Harrovian, turned to his Labour colleague Hugh Dalton, Minister for Economic Warfare, who was an old Etonian.*

Rat swimming

When informed that a Conservative MP was standing for a by-election as a Liberal:

WSC: The only instance of a rat swimming toward a sinking ship.

1905

Readable disagreement

WSC: I find [your paper] eminently readable. I entirely disagree with it!

1941 *Robert Menzies had gone to Ireland to investigate Irish neutrality, and had written a paper for the cabinet.*

Recreating the world

Chancellor Adenauer: If I were recreating the world, I would suggest that this time we not put a limit on man's intelligence without putting a limit on man's stupidity.

WSC: That would not do at all, because it would deprive me of many of my cabinet members.

1951

Red meat

Mr Gordon Walker (Labour): Does the Rt. Hon. Gentleman's answer mean that the part of 'Britain Strong and Free' which set out Conservative Party policy on the Commonwealth in the election has now been abandoned?

WSC: Nothing that we set out in our statement of policy before the election has now been abandoned, and we all look forward to the moment when we shall be able to ram red meat down the throats of Hon. Members opposite.

1952 *Labour members were asking for the beef the Conservatives had promised would follow the end of food rationing. 'Britain Strong and Free' was the 1951 Conservative Party manifesto.*

Removing MPs

Mr Schurmer (Labour): Will the Rt. Hon. Gentleman consider taking the Hon. Member for Orpington [Sir Waldron Smithers] to Bermuda with him, as it would please both sides of the House if he would take him and leave him there?

Sir Waldron Smithers (Conservative): On a point of order. May I tell you, Mr Speaker, that I take no objection to that, but I wish the Hon. Member for Sparkbrook [Mr Schurmer] would go away too.

WSC: I will try to answer that question. I earnestly hope that it will be arranged through the usual channels so that equal numbers on both sides of the House have this unfortunate experience offered to them.

1953

Ring a friend

David Lloyd George at a telephone booth: Winston, loan me a penny so I may ring a friend.

> *Churchill elaborately searched his pockets …*

WSC: Here, David, is sixpence. Now you can ring all your friends.

undated

Roman Christian communists

When Churchill asked an Italian group what party they represented, they replied: We are the Christian communists.

WSC: It must be very inspiring to your party having the catacombs so handy.

1944

Scottish dilemma

Mrs Jean Mann (Labour): Is the Prime Minister aware that … the Mint has decided to issue coins with 'Elizabeth II', and Scots who object to this title are placed in an awful dilemma?

WSC: I hope that theoretical refinements will not stop the normal conduct of business.

1953

Scottish loyalty oath

An Hon. Member: Is the Prime Minister aware that there is a strong feeling in Scotland about the oath being taken to Queen Elizabeth II on the ground of historical inaccuracy? In view of his great claim to historical accuracy himself, will he not do something to meet this very strong resentment in Scotland?

WSC: I shall be very glad to hear from the Hon. Member if he will put his question in the pillar box.

1953 *Scottish dissidents had been blowing up pillar boxes containing the new queen's royal cipher.*

Secret vs awkward

Mr De la Bere asked the prime minister to define the difference between a secret and an awkward question.

WSC: One is a danger to the country, and the other a nuisance to the government.

1940

Sidney's perch

Mr Sidney Silverman (Labour): I wonder what the Rt. Hon. Gentleman would say if he abandoned restraint.

WSC: The Hon. Gentleman is always intervening. On this occasion he did not even hop off his perch.

1949 *Silverman had very short legs, which dangled when he sat. Churchill often referred to his 'perch', especially when provoked by Silverman failing to rise to ask a question.*

Speaking volume

A Labour heckler: Speak up – don't be afraid!

WSC: I find I speak quite loud enough to silence any of *you* when I like.

1945

Speechmaking

WSC: He spoke without a note, and almost without a point.

1931 *WSC had endured a lengthy speech by Labour MP William Graham.*

Spiritual resources

Mr Gower (Conservative): Will the Prime Minister assure the House that, while we have quite properly attended to the physical needs of defence and of our other problems, we should not forget these spiritual resources which have inspired this country in the past and without which the noblest civilisation would decay?

WSC: I hardly think that that is my exclusive responsibility.

1952

Springboard, not sofa

Aneurin Bevan remarked that the Allies pondering where to go from North Africa were 'like an old man approaching a young bride: fascinated, sluggish and apprehensive'.

WSC: The army is like a peacock – nearly all tail ... I intended North Africa to be a springboard, not a sofa.

1942

Supplementary questions

Mr Shinwell (Labour): Will the Prime Minister tell us why he has suddenly become so shy? Usually he is very anxious to add a great deal on supplementary questions. Could he not expand a little on this occasion? What is the matter with him?

WSC: I have to measure the length of the response to any supplementary question by the worth, meaning and significance of that supplementary question.

1952

Toast declined

An MP suggested the House should toast, 'Death to all dictators and long life to all liberators among whom the Prime Minister is first.'

WSC: It is very early in the morning.

1944

Two gentlemen of Verona

Private secretary John Colville's Italian cook turned up six months pregnant. Said Colville: I told Winston that I believed the cook's downfall to have been brought about by a man in a street in Verona after dark.

WSC: Obviously not one of the Two Gentlemen.

1954 *WSC was referring to* The Two Gentlemen of Verona *by William Shakespeare, whose works he adored.*

Unanimously adopted

WSC: In short, we unanimously adopt the idiotic suggestion of the Minister of Production.

1940s *Oliver Lyttleton, 1st Viscount Chandos (1893–1972), Conservative MP 1940–54, Secretary of State for the Colonies 1951–4. Lyttleton opposed a bold military action because it would take two months to prepare for. WSC was infuriated, but other ministers supported Lyttleton.*

Unloved sons

WSC: Isn't it enough to have this parent volcano continually erupting in our midst? And now we are to have these subsidiary craters spouting forth the same unhealthy fumes!

1930s *Following the maiden speech of the son of an unpopular minister.*

Uproar in the opposition

WSC: ... the spectacle of a number of middle-aged gentlemen who are my political opponents being in a state of uproar and fury is really quite exhilarating to me.

1952

Virtue

Jack Seely: No, no, *mea virtute me involvo.*

WSC: Yes, you get tied up in your own virtue.

circa 1916 *WSC's friend Jack Seely, later Lord Mottistone, had a grievance with the War Office. WSC had asked why he did not bring it to the attention of the authorities.*

Welsh retorts

WSC: We have therefore appointed an Under-Secretary under the Home Office who is a Welshman, and whose name is, I believe, quite well known throughout the principality ...

Mr George Thomas (Labour, Cardiff West): Pronounce his name.

WSC: I will – Llewellyn. *Môr o gân yw Cymru i gyd* [All Wales is a sea of song].

1951[1]

Mr Hughes (Labour): Is the Rt. Hon. Gentleman aware that the Minister of Defence was absent from the first Home Guard parade last night? Is he now on open arrest awaiting court martial?

WSC: I was pursuing my studies into the Welsh language.

1951[2] *After becoming prime minister again, Churchill appointed himself Minister of Defence, as in 1940–5, although in 1952 the job was passed on. In a debate on recruitment of the Home Guard personnel, WSC was challenged by Hughes, a frequent but affectionate Welsh critic.*

Mr Hughes (Labour): Owing to the popularity the government has gained by the reduction of their salaries, is not the Prime Minister prepared to apply the principle to the big item of more than £500,000 spent on the Civil List?

WSC: *Dim o gwbl* [Nothing at all].

1951[3]

Mr Gower (Conservative): Can the Prime Minister state what course will be followed if a future British monarch should bear the name Llewellyn?

WSC: I hope I may ask for a long notice of that question.

1953[4]

Yelping

Mr George Craddock (Labour), calling out from his seat: Scandalous.

WSC: We are still allowed to debate and not merely to yelp from below the gangway.

1954 *The gangway is the aisle separating the leading members of the government or opposition from the other members, or backbenchers.*

2. Maxims and reflections

Over a long life, Churchill offered so much advice that compiling a list of his maxims is a formidable task. For this chapter I have favoured brevity, originality and, to the extent possible, remarks about a single subject. Lengthier expressions will be found in 'Churchillisms'. Retorts and comebacks, which sometimes take the form of maxims, are in 'Thrusts and parries'. Interesting expressions derived from others are in 'Great communicator'. Lines attributed to WSC but originated by others are in the Appendix.

Winston Churchill's love of English, his mastery of the language and his long parliamentary experience combined to produce maxims on human life and conduct that are singularly fascinating and continually relevant. He had deep beliefs. He stuck to them, seldom tempering his remarks for political advantage, often indeed saying quite the opposite of what a pollster might have advised him to say: a rare trait among politicians of any era.

Age

A woman is as old as she looks; a man is as old as he feels; and a boy is as old as he is treated.

1942 *WSC's comment at dinner, related by FDR's companion, Daisy Suckley, in her diaries.*

Allies

There is only one thing worse than fighting with allies, and that is fighting without them.

1945 *Quoted in Alanbrooke's Diaries. Clementine Churchill suggests a similar remark was made earlier, writing to WSC on 23 November 1943: So don't allow yourself to be made angry. I often think of your saying, that the only worse thing than Allies is not having Allies!*

Anticipation

… in life's steeplechase one must always jump the fences when they come.

1930

Anxieties

We have a lot of anxieties, and one cancels out another very often.

1943

Architecture

We shape our buildings, and afterwards our buildings shape us.

1943 *An air raid destroyed the Commons chamber on 10 May 1941. The old House was rebuilt in 1950 in its old form, insufficient to seat all members. Churchill was against 'giving each member a desk to sit at and a lid to bang' because, he explained, the House would be mostly empty most of the time; whereas, at critical votes and moments, it would fill beyond capacity, with members spilling out into the aisles, creating a suitable 'sense of crowd and urgency'.*

Bears

A bear in the forest is a proper matter for speculation; a bear in the zoo is a proper matter for public curiosity; a bear in your wife's bed is a matter of the gravest concern.

1951 *WSC to Lord Home, in respect of Stalin's appetite for expansion.*

Bombing

Learn to get used to it. Eels get used to skinning.

1940 *A wry remark added to a speech in secret session.*

Breaking vs mending

It is easier to break crockery than to mend it.

1948

Bribery
It was very much better to bribe a person than kill him, and very much better to be bribed than to be killed.
1953

Budget surplus
An announcement of a prospective surplus is always a milestone in a budget ...
1925

Capitalism and socialism
The inherent vice of capitalism is the unequal sharing of blessings. The inherent virtue of socialism is the equal sharing of miseries.
1945

Causes
Strength is granted to us all when we are needed to serve great causes.
1946[1]

We must always be ready to make sacrifices for the great causes; only in that way shall we live to keep our souls alive.
1948[2]

Change
There is nothing wrong in change, if it is in the right direction. To improve is to change, so to be perfect is to have changed often.
1925[1]

Change is agreeable to the human mind, and gives satisfaction, sometimes short-lived, to ardent and anxious public opinion.
1941[2]

Chartwell

A day away from Chartwell is a day wasted.

A frequent tribute to his home in Kent.

Chivalry in democracies

Chivalrous gallantry is not among the peculiar characteristics of excited democracy.

1899

Companions

How much easier it is to join bad companions than to shake them off!

1943 *Referring to the fall of Mussolini a few weeks earlier, and Italy's having been misled by false guides.*

Conferences

Hope flies on wings, and international conferences plod afterwards along dusty roads.

1925

Conscience

Conscience and muddle cannot be reconciled; conscience apart from truth is mere stupidity ...

1948

Contrast

The glory of light cannot exist without its shadows.

1931

Courage

Courage is rightly esteemed the first of human qualities because, as has been said, it is the quality which guarantees all others.

1931 *'As has been said' refers to Samuel Johnson's '... Sir, you know courage is reckoned the greatest of all virtues; because, unless a man has that virtue, he has no security for preserving any other.'*

Criticism

Criticism in the body politic is like pain in the human body. It is not pleasant, but where would the body be without it?

1940

Danger

Dangers which are warded off and difficulties which are overcome before they reach a crisis are utterly unrecognised. Eaten bread is soon forgotten.

1919[1]

When danger is far off we may think of our weakness; when it is near we must not forget our strength.

1939[2]

Dealing in guineas

Those who dealt in guineas were not usually of the impoverished class.

1903 *The guinea coin, first struck in 1664 from gold obtained from Guinea, was originally 30 shillings, then, from 1717, 21 shillings or one pound and one shilling, and was commonly used by the upper classes or in adverts pitched towards them.*

Death

Wait and see how you feel when the tide is running the other way. It does not seem so easy to die when death is near.

1899[1] *WSC to a Boer soldier who said he would fight for ever.*

Death is the greatest gift that God has made to us.

1943[2]

Death in politics

In war you can only be killed once, but in politics many times.

circa 1904 *Tentatively included as likely, but not proven. Halle references a 1902 newspaper interview, but provides no title or date. Manchester footnotes a non-existent entry in the official biography document volumes when WSC supposedly said this to a reporter in spring 1904, just before he quit the Conservatives for the Liberals.*

Deeds and consequences

The advantage and significance of deeds is that they bring consequences.

1949

Democracy

Democracy is more vindictive than cabinets.

1901

Denial

Some people will deny anything, but there are some denials that do not alter the facts.

1910

Despair

It is a crime to despair. We must learn to draw from misfortune the means of future strength.

1938

Destiny

Only one link in the chain of destiny can be handled at a time.

1945

Difficulties

Difficulties must not affright us. If some stand out, all the more must the others be banded together.

1936[1] *WSC would be bewildered by the modern habit of substituting the word 'issues' for 'difficulties'. He knew exactly what difficulties were, and he stood no nonsense from them.*

Don't argue the matter. The difficulties will argue for themselves.

1941[2] *Prime Minister to Chief of Combined Operations: Churchill's first directive on what became the Mulberry Harbours used in the Normandy invasion of 1944: 'They must float up and down with the tide …'*

Diplomatic relations

The reason for having diplomatic relations is not to confer a compliment, but to secure a convenience.

1949

Disinterest

Rare and precious is the truly disinterested man.

1899

Doing nothing

Things do not get better by being let alone. Unless they are adjusted, they explode with a shattering detonation.

1927 *Contrary advice to Volume I of* The World Crisis; *WSC is oversimplifying.*

Doing our best

… how little we should worry about anything except doing our best.

1951

Doing without

So we have had to dispense with the indispensable.

1922

Dual control

Dual control is two persons attempting to control one thing. The reverse process is one person attempting to control two things.

1920

Empires of the mind

The empires of the future are the empires of the mind.

1943

Energy

... energy of mind does not depend on energy of body ... energy should be exercised and not exhausted.

1944

Engineers

We need a lot of engineers in the modern world, but we do not want a world of modern engineers.

1948

Evil

It is an important thing to diagnose the evil, but unless the malady be recognised it is idle to attempt to seek the remedy.

1926[1]

Evils can be created much quicker than they can be cured.

1951[2]

Facts

You must look at facts, because they look at you.

1925[1]

Facts are better than dreams.

1948[2] *On taking office as prime minister, 10 May 1940.*

United wishes and goodwill cannot overcome brute facts.
1951[3]

Failure

Even [man's] greatest neglects or failures may bring him good.
Even his greatest achievements may work him ill.
1936

Fate

What a slender thread the greatest of things can hang by.
1940

Finance

In finance, everything that is agreeable is unsound and
everything that is sound is disagreeable.
1926

Foresight

Plant a garden in which you can sit when digging days are done.
1921[1]

When you are leaving for an unknown destination it is a good
plan to attach a restaurant car at the tail of the train.
1922[2]

How little can we foresee the consequences either of wise or
unwise action, of virtue or of malice!
1948[3] *WSC added: 'Without this measureless and perpetual uncertainty, the
drama of human life would be destroyed.'*

Fortune

Sometimes when [Fortune] scowls most spitefully, she is
preparing her most dazzling gifts.
1931

Free market

If you destroy a free market you create a black market.

1949 *He added: If you have 10,000 regulations you destroy all respect for the law.*

Friendship

One always measures friendships by how they show up in bad weather.

1948

Fright

… it is much better to be frightened now than to be killed hereafter.

1934

Future

The future is unknowable, but the past should give us hope.

1958

German enemy

A Hun alive is a war in prospect.

1940

Give us the tools

Give us the tools, and we will finish the job.

1941 *Addressing the USA and Roosevelt, referring to the Lend-Lease Act.*

Great men

One mark of a great man is the power of making lasting impressions upon people he meets.

1930[1]

Often in the casual remarks of great men one learns their true mind in an intimate way.

1936[2]

Harsh laws

Harsh laws are at times better than no laws at all.

1906

Hatred

Hatred plays the same part in government as acids in chemistry.

1929

Help vs harm

Help each other when you can, but never harm.

1938

High ground

Do not quit the heights.

1943

Hindsight

After things are over it is easy to choose the fine mental and moral positions which one should adopt.

1950

History

Persevere towards those objectives which are lighted for us by all the wisdom and inspiration of the past.

1948

Honours

Honours should go where death and danger go ...

1916

Hope

Nourish your hopes, but do not overlook realities.

1935

Hot topics
When you have to hold a hot coffee pot, it is better not to break the handle off ...
1944

Hypocrisy
Few people practise what they preach ...
1929

Idealism
No folly is more costly than the folly of intolerant idealism.
1929

Ideas
Ideas acquire a momentum of their own.
1927

Ifs
We live in a world of 'ifs'.
1899

Imagination
... imagination without deep and full knowledge is a snare ...
1950

Imperialism
... imperialism and economics clash as often as honesty and self-interest.
1898[1]

I have always noticed that whenever a radical takes to Imperialism he catches it in a very acute form.
1901[2] *Sir Charles Dilke (1843–1911), a Liberal Imperialist, had come out in favour of an increase in Army estimates.*

Impulse

Almost the chief mystery of life is what makes one do things.

1931

Innovation

We must beware of needless innovation, especially when guided by logic.

1942

Invitations

It is a very fine thing to refuse an invitation, but it is a good thing to wait till you get it first.

1911

Jaw to jaw

Meeting jaw to jaw is better than war.

1954 *Commonly misquoted as 'Jaw, jaw is better than war, war,' an expression coined four years later by Prime Minister Harold Macmillan, on a visit to Australia.*

Judgment

We shall not be judged by the criticisms of our opponents but by the consequences of our acts.

1926

Justice

The first maxim of English jurisprudence is that complainers should come into Court with clean hands.

1914[1]

Justice moves slowly and remorselessly upon its path, but it reaches its goal eventually.

1929[2]

One ought to be just before one is generous.
1947[3]

KBO
We must just KBO.

1941 *WSC to private secretary John Peck. Churchill's familiar maxim, usually delivered to colleagues and family, and abbreviated in polite company. It stood for 'Keep Buggering On'.*

King vs ace
The king cannot fall unworthily if he falls to the sword of the ace.

1912 *WSC to Edward Marsh as he lost a king in a trick.*

Languages
The recognition of their language is precious to a small people.

1906 *From a speech in favour of ratifying the Transvaal constitution, recognising the Boer language, which he considered magnanimous to the Boer inhabitants.*

Libraries
Nothing makes a man more reverent than a library.
1921

Life
Usually youth is for freedom and reform, maturity for judicious compromise, and old age for stability and repose.
1927[1]

The journey has been enjoyable and well worth the taking – once.
1931[2]

… live dangerously; take things as they come; dread naught, all will be well.
1932[3]

Luck

Men may make mistakes, and learn from their mistakes. Men may have bad luck, and their luck may change.

1942

Magnanimity

As we have triumphed, so we may be merciful; as we are strong, so we can afford to be generous.

1906[1] *An example of WSC's consistency: forty years later it was 'In victory, magnanimity.'*

… you don't want to knock a man down except to pick him up in a better frame of mind.

1949[2]

Man is spirit.

1955 *WSC's final words to his non-cabinet ministers upon his retirement as prime minister, according to Lord De L'Isle and Dudley, as quoted by Martin Gilbert.*

Mankind

… human beings may be divided into three classes: those who are billed to death, those who are worried to death, and those who are bored to death.

1925[1]

Man is a land animal. Even rabbits are allowed to have warrens, and foxes have earths.

1946[2]

The power of man has grown in every sphere except over himself.

1953[3] *Lady Churchill read this acceptance speech of the Nobel Prize for Literature, at the award ceremony for which she represented her husband. Churchill was in Bermuda conferring with President Eisenhower and French Premier Laniel.*

Martyrdom

They could not have martyrdom without the accessories of the faggot and the stake, and if a man made his protest he ought to be prepared to pay the price.

1904

Milk into babies

There is no finer investment for any community than putting milk into babies.

1943 *WSC recycled and improved this maxim from a remark he made at the City Carlton Club on 28 June 1939: 'There is no more far-seeing investment for a nation than to put milk, food and education into young children.'*

Mind as rifle

Don't turn your mind into an ammunition wagon, but turn it into a rifle to fire off other people's ammunition.

1900 *Churchill's advice to his cousin Shane Leslie at Eton, before WSC left for his American/Canadian lecture tour.*

Moral force

Moral force is, unhappily, no substitute for armed force, but it is a very great reinforcement ...

1937

Myths

At times of crisis, myths have their historical importance.

1940 *WSC to Bill Deakin, his literary assistant on WSC's* A History of the English-Speaking Peoples. *See 'Stories and jokes: King Alfred and the burnt cakes'.*

National borrowing

When you borrow money from another country for the sacred purpose of national rehabilitation, it is wrong to squander it upon indulgences.

1947

National collapse

When a country collapses, the chaos reproduces itself in every microcosm.

1941 *Private Secetary Eddie Marsh: Winston was in great form ... talking of the difficulties among the Free French.*

National conscience

A nation without a conscience is a nation without a soul.
A nation without a soul is a nation that cannot live.

1951

Nature

Nature will not be admired by proxy.

1898 *WSC gave this as the reason for not describing the night-time beauty of the North-west frontier of India.*

Necessity

It is no use saying, 'We are doing our best.' You have got to succeed in doing what is necessary.

1916

Negotiations

Quit murdering and start arguing.

1920 *WSC to his cousin Shane Leslie, who asked what advice Churchill would give to Sinn Fein in Ireland.*

News making

It is better to be making the news than taking it; to be an actor rather than a critic.

1898

Old and new

Do not let spacious plans for a new world divert your energies from saving what is left of the old.

1941 *Prime Minister to Minister of Public Works and Buildings.*

Opportunity

... everyone has his day, and some days last longer than others.
1952

Parliament

The object of Parliament is to substitute argument for fisticuffs.
1951

Peacekeeping

I would rather have a peacekeeping hypocrisy than straightforward, brazen vice, taking the form of unlimited war.
1937

Perfection

The maxim 'Nothing avails but perfection' may be spelt shorter: 'Paralysis.'
1942[1]

... perfect solutions to our difficulties are not to be looked for in an imperfect world ...
1951[2]

Perseverance

When one crest line is abandoned it is necessary to return to the next. Halting at a 'halfway house' midway in the valley is fatal.
1906[1]

We must go on and on like the gun-horses, till we drop.
1940s[2] *WSC to a wartime secretary, Elizabeth Nel: '... he stopped once to ask if I were tired, and when I told him I was not, he said [this].'*

Continue to pester, nag, and bite.
1941[3] *WSC to Sir Ronald Campbell, British representative in Belgrade, urging him to continue attempting to convince Yugoslavia to stand with Greece against the Germans.*

We must learn to be equally good at what is short and sharp and what is long and tough.

1941[4]

… never give in, never, never, never, never – in nothing, great or small, large or petty – never give in except to convictions of honour and good sense.

1941[5] *It is sometimes said that Churchill once gave a three-word speech: 'Never give in.' The speech containing these words, about twenty minutes long, was given to the boys at his old school, Harrow, during the first of many visits in his later years.*

Personal relations

There is all the difference in the world between a man who knocks you down and a man who leaves you alone.

1944

Personnel

You should never harness a thoroughbred to a dung cart.

1942 *WSC to Minister of Information Brendan Bracken, who had replaced Alfred Duff Cooper (present on this occasion) in July 1941. WSC meant that the minister is dealing constantly with the press, and must confront a number of disagreeable practices and people.*

Pleasure

… when one is trying to give pleasure it is always well to do it in the best possible way.

1951

Political action

In politics when you are in doubt what to do, do nothing … when you are in doubt what to say, say what you really think.

1905

Politicians

Politicians rise by toils and struggles. They expect to fall; they hope to rise again.

1931

Politics

It is a fine game to play the game of politics and it is well worth a good hand before really plunging.

1895

Power

Where there is great power there is great responsibility ... where there is no power there can, I think, be no responsibility.

1906[1]

The finest combination in the world is power and mercy. The worst combination in the world is weakness and strife.

1919[2]

It is certainly more agreeable to have the power to give than to receive.

1949[3]

But on the whole it is wise in human affairs, and in the government of men, to separate pomp from power.

1952[4]

Principles

It is always more easy to discover and proclaim general principles than to apply them.

1936[1] *Private address to the Conservative Members' Committee on Foreign Affairs, dated 'the end of March'.*

People who are not prepared to do unpopular things and to defy clamour are not fit to be ministers in times of stress.

1943² *Churchill was commenting favourably on the cabinet's decision to support the Home Secretary, Herbert Morrison, in releasing the Mosleys from prison. Sir Oswald and Lady Mosley had been imprisoned at the outset of the war for suspected fascist leanings.*

In critical and baffling situations it is always best to recur to first principles and simple action.

1951³

Prophets
A hopeful disposition is not the sole qualification to be a prophet.

1927

Quarrels
The worst quarrels only arise when both sides are equally in the right and in the wrong.

1936

Recrimination
… the use of recriminating about the past [is] to enforce effective action at the present.

1936¹ *Four years later, by then in charge, Churchill took a different approach; see next entries.*

We are not in a position to say tonight, 'The past is the past.' We cannot say, 'The past is the past,' without surrendering the future.

1938²

… if we open a quarrel between the past and the present we shall find that we have lost the future.

1940³

Redress of grievances

... the redress of the grievances of the vanquished should precede the disarmament of the victors.

1935

Repetition

In the problems which the Almighty sets His humble servants things hardly ever happen the same way twice over ...

1948 *For contradictory advice see 'War wounds' below.*

Resources

The sledge is bare of babies, and though the pack may crunch the driver's bones, the winter will not be ended.

1914

Retrospect

We cannot undo the past, but we are bound to pass it in review in order to draw from it such lessons as may be applicable to the future ...

1936[1]

The longer you can look back, the farther you can look forward.

1944[2] *Often misquoted.*

Right and consistent

... it is better to be both right and consistent. But if you have to choose – you must choose to be right.

1952

Right and hard

Things are not always right because they are hard, but if they are right one must not mind if they are also hard.

1948

Right and honest

It is a fine thing to be honest, but it is very important for a Prime Minister to be right.

1923

Right and irresponsible

Perhaps it is better to be irresponsible and right than to be responsible and wrong.

1950 *Prime Minister Attlee had called WSC irresponsible for suggesting that Germany contribute to the defence of Western Europe.*

Right and wrong

Except in so far as force is concerned, there is no equality between right and wrong.

1945

Risk

You must put your head into the lion's mouth if the performance is to be a success.

1900

Safety

To try to be safe everywhere is to be strong nowhere.

1951

Satisfaction

How often in life must one be content with what one can get!

1943

Secrets

... it is wonderful how well men can keep secrets they have not been told ...

1900

Settlements

The best evidence of the fairness of any settlement is the fact that it fully satisfies neither party.

1926[1]

It is a sort of British idea that when you reach agreement you take the rough with the smooth.

1948[2]

Shot at without result

Nothing in life is so exhilarating as to be shot at without result.

1898 *Famously quoted by a well-read Churchillian, President Ronald Reagan, after surviving an assassin's bullet in 1981.*

Simplicity

Out of intense complexities, intense simplicities emerge.

1927[1]

Life, which is so complicated and difficult in great matters, nearly always presents itself in simple terms.

1941[2]

All the greatest things are simple, and many can be expressed in a single word: Freedom; Justice; Honour; Duty; Mercy; Hope.

1947[3]

Slothfulness

Let not the slothful chortle.

1940s *Lord Mountbatten to the Edmonton Churchill Society, 1966.*

Social reform

All social reform ... which is not founded upon a stable medium of internal exchange becomes a swindle and a fraud.

1947

Solvency

Solvency is valueless without security, and security is impossible to achieve without solvency.

1953

Speechmaking

It is pretty tough to reshape human society in an after-dinner speech.

1941 *Response to the draft of a long after-dinner speech which Halifax, the British ambassador in Washington, was planning to give.*

Spite

Nothing should be done for spite's sake.

1944

Success

Success always demands a greater effort.

1940

Sufficiency

Enough is as good as a feast.

1918 *Probably not truly original but not tracked to another source.*

Temptations

Would you be strong morally or physically? You must resist temptations.

1898

Theory and practice

Concede the theory and you have no trouble in practice.

1945 *On allowing women to become members of parliament.*

Thought

After all, a man's Life must be nailed to a cross of either Thought or Action.

1930[1]

One can usually put one's thoughts better in one's own words.

1940[2]

Thought arising from factual experience may be a bridle or a spur.

1952[3]

Thrift

It is a great mistake to suppose that thrift is caused only by fear; it springs from hope as well as from fear; where there is no hope, be sure there will be no thrift.

1908

Tidiness and symmetry

Tidiness is a virtue, symmetry is often a constituent of beauty …

1945

Time

Time and money are largely interchangeable terms.

1926[1]

No one should waste a day.

1948[2]

Tributes

… a favourable verdict is always to be valued, even if it comes from an unjust judge or a nobbled umpire.

1931 *During the 1931 budget debate, Lloyd George and the Liberals had praised Churchill's previous administration of the exchequer (1924–9).*

Trust

In stormy weather one must trust to the man at the helm ...
1900

Truth

This truth is incontrovertible. Panic may resent it, ignorance may deride it, malice may distort it, but there it is.
1916[1]

... if truth is many-sided, mendacity is many-tongued ...
1940[2] *WSC was defending the government in the failing Norwegian campaign.*

In wartime, Truth is so precious that she should always be attended by a bodyguard of lies.
1943[3] *WSC uttered this famous line when Stalin approved of issuing fake invasion plans. Thus 'Operation Bodyguard' became the name for deception plans for 'Overlord', the 1944 invasion of France.*

Let no one swerve off the high road of truth and honour.
1945[4]

The dominant forces in human history have come from the perception of great truths and the faithful pursuance of great causes.
1950[5]

Tyranny

Always be on guard against tyranny, whatever shape it may assume.
1945

Unexpected

The element of the unexpected and the unforeseeable ... saves us from falling into the mechanical thraldom of the logicians.
1946

Unteachable mankind

Unteachable from infancy to tomb – there is the first and main characteristic of mankind.

1928 *Letter to Lord Beaverbrook after reading Beaverbrook's* Politicians and the War. *In Virginia in 1946 WSC told the state General Assembly: 'It has been said that the dominant lesson of history is that mankind is unteachable.'*

Vanquished enemies

If you want your horse to pull your wagon, you have to give him some hay.

1945

Vengeance

Nothing is more costly, nothing is more sterile, than vengeance.

1946[1]

Vengeance is the most costly and dissipating of luxuries.

1948[2]

Virtue vs wickedness

Virtuous motives, trammelled by inertia and timidity, are no match for armed and resolute wickedness.

1948

Virtuous circle

[Tax relief] will substitute a virtuous circle for the vicious circle.

1928

War and democracy

We have had nothing else but wars since democracy took charge.

1947 *This remark displays more a regret over the slaughter in the first half of the 20th century than any regret over democracy, which he always supported.*

War and peace

... those who can win a war well can rarely make a good peace, and those who could make a good peace would never have won the war. It would perhaps be pressing the argument too far to suggest that I could do both.

1930

War wounds

Nobody is ever wounded twice on the same day.

1899 *Churchill said this to the engineer of the armoured train when ambushed by the Boers near Chieveley, Natal. He later recommended the engineer, who stayed calm and eventually drove the locomotive away, for the Albert Medal.*

Weakness and treason

Weakness is not treason, though it may be equally disastrous.

1948

Wealth and commonwealth

To hunt wealth is not to capture commonwealth.

1934[1]

The production of new wealth must precede commonwealth, otherwise there will only be common poverty.

1945[2]

You may try to destroy wealth, and find that all you have done is to increase poverty.

1947[3]

Wicked and dictators

The wicked are not always clever, nor are dictators always right.

1950

Win or lose

If we win, nobody will care. If we lose, there will be nobody
to care.

1941

Wisdom

All wisdom is not new wisdom.

1938[1] *Churchill used the maxim several times in his speeches from 1938 to
1947; this is the first appearance.*

It would be great reform in politics if wisdom could be made to
spread as easily and as rapidly as folly.

1947[2]

Women

It is hard, if not impossible, to snub a beautiful woman; they
remain beautiful and the rebuke recoils.

1900

Work

It is no use doing what you like; you have got to like what
you do.

1925[1]

Many things are learnt by those who live their whole lives with
their main work …

1928[2]

World War II: 1940

But nothing surpasses 1940.

1949

World War II: Moral

In war, Resolution. In defeat, Defiance. In victory, Magnanimity.
In peace, Goodwill.

1930 Churchill first published this moral in his 1930 autobiography, stating that he had offered it for a war memorial in France, but that it was not accepted. He did not forget, and deployed it as the moral for his WW2 memoirs. The first phrase was originally 'In war, Fury'.

Wrongdoing

... it is always very difficult to know, when you embark on the path of wrongdoing, exactly where to stop.
1911

Youth

... Youth, Youth, Youth; efficient youth marching forward from service in the field ...

1944 Misquoted by Harold Nicolson in his diary as 'Youth, youth, youth and renovation, energy, boundless energy'.

3. Stories and jokes

Churchill was no fountain of tales, in the way that Presidents Truman and Reagan were – but when he told a tale it was often memorable. His most revealing composition was his bitter-sweet 1947 short story 'The Dream'. When Lady Thatcher was presented with a limited edition of 'The Dream' by the Churchill Centre in 1993, she said she stayed up late one night, reading and pondering it: 'I was totally fascinated by the imagination of the story, and how much it reveals of Winston the man and the son.'

On occasion Churchill was, however, an inventive storyteller. Taxed over repeating the unprovable myth of King Alfred and the burnt cakes, he responded that in times of crisis, 'myths have their historical importance'. He wrote one novel and several short stories, which have their merits along with their flaws. Of his novel *Savrola*, WSC wrote, 'I have consistently urged my friends to abstain from reading it.'

Bear, buffalo and donkey

I realised at Teheran for the first time what a small nation we are. There I sat with the great Russian bear on one side of me, with paws outstretched, and on the other side the great American buffalo, and between the two sat the poor little English donkey who was the only one, the only one of the three, who knew the right way home.

1944 *WSC to Violet Bonham Carter, eight months after the Teheran conference.*

Disarmament fable

Once upon a time all the animals in the Zoo decided that they would disarm, and they arranged to have a conference to arrange the matter. So the Rhinoceros said when he opened the proceedings that the use of teeth was barbarous and horrible and ought to be strictly prohibited by general consent. Horns, which were mainly defensive weapons, would, of course, have to be allowed. The Buffalo, the Stag, the Porcupine, and even the little Hedgehog all said they would vote with the Rhino, but the Lion and the Tiger took a different view. They defended teeth and even claws, which they described as honourable weapons of immemorial antiquity. The Panther, the Leopard, the Puma, and the whole tribe of small cats all supported the Lion and the Tiger. Then the Bear spoke. He proposed that both teeth and horns should be banned and never used again for fighting by any animal. It would be quite enough if animals were allowed to give each other a good hug when they quarrelled. No one could object to that. It was so fraternal, and that would be a great step towards peace. However, all the other animals were very offended with the Bear, and the Turkey fell into a perfect panic. The discussion got so hot and angry, and all those animals began thinking so much about horns and teeth and hugging when they argued about the peaceful intentions that had brought them together that they began to look at one another in a very nasty way. Luckily the keepers were able to calm them down and persuade them to go back quietly to their cages, and they began to feel quite friendly with one another again.

1928

Ignorance

When I hear people talking in an airy way of throwing modern armies ashore here and there as if they were bales of goods to be dumped on a beach and forgotten, I really marvel at the lack of knowledge which still prevails of the conditions of modern war ... [Critics also remind me of] the sailor who jumped into a dock to rescue a small boy from drowning. About a week later this sailor was accosted by a woman who asked, 'Are you the man who picked my son out of the water the other night?' The sailor replied modestly, 'That is true, ma'am.' 'Ah,' said the woman, 'you are the man I am looking for. Where is his cap?'

1943

King Alfred and the burnt cakes

The story of Alfred is made known to us in some detail in the pages of Asser, a monk of St David's, who became Bishop of Sherborne ... We see the warrior-king disguised as a minstrel harping in the Danish camps. We see him acting as a kitchen-boy to a Saxon housewife. The celebrated story of Alfred and the Cakes first appears in a late edition of Bishop Asser's Life. It runs: It happened one day that the countrywoman, who was the wife of the cowherd with whom King Alfred was staying, was going to bake bread, and the King was sitting by the fireside making ready his bow and arrows and other weapons. A moment came when the woman saw that her bread was burning; she rushed up and removed it from the fire, upbraiding the undaunted King with these words (recorded, strangely, in the original in Latin hexameters): 'Alack, man, why have you not turned over the bread when you see that it is burning, especially as you so much like eating it hot?' The misguided woman little thought that she was talking to King Alfred, who had fought so vigorously against the heathens and won so many victories over them.

1956[1]

... at times of crisis, myths have their historical importance: the cakes symbolise a myth of British resistance in their sternest hour against the foreign invader, and were the source of inspiration to those dim distant figures, the Counts of the Saxon shore, striving to defend the island.

1940[2] *Literary assistant Bill Deakin had asked WSC why he was including Bishop Asser's myth in his* A History of the English-Speaking Peoples.

Making certain

As the man whose mother-in-law had died in Brazil replied, when asked how the remains should be disposed of, 'Embalm, cremate and bury. Take no risks!'

1938

Norman from Saxon

One summer evening … Gurth the Swineherd and Wamba the Jester [were] fresh from their famous colloquy on the curious fact that oxen, pigs and sheep, which were Saxons while they lived and had to be tended, were, when the time came to cook them, transformed in death into Norman beef, pork and mutton, and thus qualified to figure on noble boards.

1933

Objections

I remember it was the fashion in the army when a court martial was being held and the prisoner was brought in, that he should be asked if he objected to being tried by the president or to any of those officers who composed the court martial. On one occasion a prisoner was so insubordinate as to answer, 'I object to the whole bloody lot of you.'

1927 *The word 'bloody', not permitted in parliamentary discourse in 1927, is represented by a long dash in Hansard.*

Optimists and pessimists

We remember the sardonic wartime joke about the optimist and the pessimist. The optimist was the man who did not mind what happened so long as it did not happen to him. The pessimist was the man who lived with the optimist.

1938

Powder to the bear

I have often tried to set down the strategic truths I have comprehended in the form of simple anecdotes, and they rank this way in my mind. One of them is the celebrated tale of the man who gave the powder to the bear. He mixed the powder with the greatest care, making sure that not only the ingredients but the proportions were absolutely correct. He rolled it up in a large paper spill, and was about to blow it down the bear's throat. *But the bear blew first.*

1951 *Exactly what the powder was, WSC left to his listeners. But, since he said this in the context of his warning to General Auchinleck that the Germans might attack first in Africa, he certainly meant it to be helpful advice.*

Precision in language

A man called Thomson went to a surgeon and asked him to castrate him. The surgeon demurred, but when the man persisted and argued he eventually agreed, and took him into hospital. The morning after the operation Thomson woke up in great discomfort. He noticed that the man in the next bed was in pain and was groaning. He leant towards him over the side of the bed. 'What did they do to you,' he called. The man replied: 'I've been circumcised.' 'Good Lord,' Thomson exclaimed, 'that's the word I couldn't remember when the surgeon asked me what I wanted done.'

1944

Spanish prisoner

I believe we have been all these months in the position of the Spanish prisoner who languished for twenty years in a dungeon until one morning the idea struck him to push the door, which had been open all the time.

1915 *WSC to Arthur Balfour, his successor at the Admiralty, arguing for a renewal of the naval attack on the Dardanelles.*

St George and the dragon

[Nowadays] St George would arrive in Cappadocia accompanied not by a horse, but by a secretariat. He would be armed not with a lance, but with several flexible formulas. He would, of course, be welcomed by the local branch of the League of Nations Union. He would propose a conference with the dragon – a Round Table Conference, no doubt, that would be more convenient for the dragon's tail. He would make a trade agreement with the dragon. He would lend the dragon a lot of money of the Cappadocian taxpayers. The maiden's release would be referred to Geneva, the dragon reserving all his rights meanwhile. Finally, St George would be photographed with the dragon (inset – the maiden).

1933 WSC was mocking what he saw as the easy mark Britain was becoming in international negotiations: a remark which certainly has its applications today.

Stag and Hounds

Last night the Hon. Member for Bilston [Mr Will Nally] drew an affecting picture of my personal position; the noble stag was dying, the curs were at his throat: his own friends behind him were hogs … the hounds, as the Hon. Member for Bilston put it, do not worry me … I must say that the maiden glance of the Hon. Member for Bilston at the House of Commons should impress us somewhat with the unfavourable impression we produce upon him. Here are hogs, there are hounds. I trust that the longer experience of this Chamber will make him realise that both these branches of the animal kingdom have their virtues.

1945

The Dream

One foggy afternoon in November 1947 I was painting in my studio at the cottage down the hill at Chartwell. Someone had sent me a portrait of my father … The canvas had been badly torn, and though I am very shy of painting human faces I thought I would try to make a copy of it … I was just trying to give the twirl to his moustache when I suddenly felt an odd sensation. I turned round with my palette in my hand, and there, sitting in my red leather upright armchair, was my father. He looked just as I had seen him in his prime … 'What year is it? [he said.] I don't remember anything after ninety-four. I was very confused that year … So more than fifty years have passed. A lot must have happened.' 'It has indeed, Papa.' 'Tell me about it.' [Winston recounts the sad history of 1895–1947.] 'Winston, you have told me a terrible tale. I would never have believed that such things could happen. I am glad I did not live to see them. As I listened to you unfolding these fearful facts you seemed to know a great deal about them. I never expected that you would develop so far and so fully. Of course you are too old now to think about such things, but when I hear you talk I really wonder you didn't go into politics. You might have done a lot to help. You might even have made a name for yourself.' He gave me a benignant smile. He then took the match to light his cigarette and struck it. There was a tiny flash. He vanished. The chair was empty. The illusion had passed. I rubbed my brush again in my paint, and turned to finish the moustache. But so vivid had my fancy been that I felt too tired to go on. Also my cigar had gone out, and the ash had fallen among all the paints.

1947 *There is room here only for the very beginning and end of 'The Dream'. It is part of the artistry of this imaginary, wistfully beautiful story that Winston's father, briefly brought back to life aged about forty-five, is never allowed to know what his 74-year-old son has accomplished. Other quotations from 'The Dream' are in other chapters.*

4. Churchillisms

Churchill's love of English was agreeably expressed in words and expressions he created, or old lines to which he gave new life. All those herein are ones he invented, including Battle of the Bulge, Minimum Standard and Naval Holiday.

Old words, he said, were the best of all, and he indulged in them: correctitude, palimpsest, parlementaire, guttersnipe, purblind. If a word didn't exist to suit him, he would invent one: paintatious, improvose, Namsosed, bottlescape. Churchill would also create new words out of common ones: 're-rat' for deserting your party the second time, 'fearthought' for futile worrying.

His usage was whimsical as well as inventive, as for example when he named his hen coop 'Chickenham Palace'; or when he compared people to llamas, eagles, bulldogs, pugs and bees; or used their names to describe their functions: his chauffeur Bullock drove 'the bullock cart'. Playing on names was a hobby: 'Can'tellopoulos' for Greek Prime Minister Kanellopoulos. Thanks to Churchill, the name of Norway's fascist ruler, Quisling, entered dictionaries as a synonym for traitor.

Afterlight
Judged in afterlight these views can hardly be contested.
1923

All for Al
Al for All, and All for Al.
1928 *Alfred E. Smith (1873–1944), four-term Governor of New York, Democratic presidential candidate, 1928. Churchill offered this slogan to Bernard Baruch for Smith's campaign.*

Anticipatory plagiarism

Mr Lowe seems to have been walking over my footsteps before I had trodden them, because he said, trying to explain what had occurred to the satisfaction of a very strict House in those days: 'And so each year will take money from its successor, and this process may go on till the end of time, although how it will be settled when the world comes to an end I am at a loss to know.' It was unconscious anticipatory plagiarism.

1927 *A droll way to admit someone had an idea before you. Robert Lowe, First Viscount Sherbrooke (1811–1892), Liberal MP (1852–80), Gladstone's Chancellor of the Exchequer, 1868–73.*

Battle of the Bulge

Evidently this battle will be known as the Battle of the Bulge.

1940 *This remark preceded by over four years Hitler's attempted breakout, in the selfsame Ardennes Forest, in 1944. WSC said this to French General Gamelin, slapping him 'heartily on the shoulder (the General winced)', according to General Ismay. Churchill did not recall the French term for 'bulge' (saillant) and satisfied himself with 'boolge'.*

Blood, toil, tears and sweat

I have nothing to offer but blood, toil, tears and sweat.

1940 *This phrase had a long gestation: Churchill was evolving early versions of it in 1900, and in 1611 the poet John Donne had written of '… thy Teares, or Sweat, or Bloud'.*

Bloodthirsty guttersnipe

So now this bloodthirsty guttersnipe must launch his mechanised armies upon new fields of slaughter, pillage and devastation.

1941 *Broadcast the night of Hitler's invasion of Russia; WSC, despite a lifetime aversion to communism, immediately promised all possible British aid to Russia.*

Boneless Wonder

I remember when I was a child, being taken to the celebrated Barnum's circus, which contained an exhibition of freaks and monstrosities, but the exhibit ... which I most desired to see was the one described as 'The Boneless Wonder'. My parents judged that that spectacle would be too revolting and demoralising for my youthful eyes, and I have waited fifty years to see the Boneless Wonder [Prime Minister Ramsay MacDonald] sitting on the Treasury Bench.

1931

Bottlescape

This is my bottlescape.

This was a title for his famous still life of bottles, which Churchill had commanded the children to round up for his brush.

British restaurants

I hope the term 'Communal Feeding Centres' is not going to be adopted. It is an odious expression, suggestive of Communism and the workhouse. I suggest you call them 'British Restaurants'. Everybody associates the word 'restaurant' with a good meal, and they may as well have the name if they cannot get anything else.

1941 *WSC to Minister of Food.*

Bullock cart

I think I'll have the Bullock cart.

1950s *A Humber limousine from the government pool, driven by a chauffeur named Bullock, usually carried Churchill back and forth to London.*

Byss

I had a feeling once about Mathematics, that I saw it all – Depth beyond depth was revealed to me – the Byss and the Abyss. I saw, as one might see the transit of Venus – or even the Lord Mayor's Show, a quantity passing through infinity and changing its sign from plus to minus. I saw exactly how it happened and why the tergiversation was inevitable: and how the one step involved all the others. It was like politics. But it was after dinner and I let it go!

1930

Camels and gnats

I have heard of people aiming at a gnat and swallowing a camel, but I have never before heard of people who, having already swallowed a camel, come forward and plead that their gullets are not sufficiently expansive to accommodate a gnat.

1910 *Churchill was moving a modest amendment to a major bill. The phrase may not originate with WSC, but he liked it well enough to repeat it at least twice over the next 30 years.*

Can'tellopoulus

Kanellopoulos, Can'tellopoulos, Kanellopoulous … All right. I'll see him!

1942 *Panagiotis Kanellopoulos (1902–1986), Greek prime minister, 1945 and 1967. WSC, ever regretting finding time for this interview, replied whenever approached by his private secretary: 'Can't-ellopoulos!'*

Cheeked, abused and girded

Britain has always floated upon her Navy. Her great Indian Empire has gone down one drain, and now the Admiralty proclaims that the British Home Fleet has gone down another. Can you wonder, with these weapons, that you are cheeked by Chile, abused by the Argentine and girded at by Guatemala?

1948 *A fine example of alliteration, as WSC protested the diminution of the Royal Navy by the post-war Labour Government.*

Chickenham Palace

It's called Chickenham Palace. [Then, pointing to a 'noisome and messy little piece of bare ground':] And that is Chickenham Palace Gardens.

1949 *Sir Archibald Sinclair recalled: He took me around the farms, showed me shorthorns and Jerseys and then a brick hen house he had built himself*

... 'What kind of hens?' I asked. 'Oh, I don't bother about the details,' growled Winston.

Choate

How could the peoples know? ... What choate and integral conviction could they form?

1929 *A. L. Rowse wrote: Eddie [Marsh] brought down an infuriated mob of grammarians upon Winston's head by passing the word 'choate' which the latter deemed to exist: 'inchoate' existed, what more natural than to suppose therefore that there must be a word 'choate'?*

Chumbolly

The Chumbolly must do his duty and help you with your milk, you are to tell him so from me. At his age greediness and even swinishness at table are virtues.

1911 *WSC to Clementine ('my precious pussy cat') shortly after the birth of his son Randolph, to whom they gave this evocative nickname.*

Clatter and buzz, gape and gloat

A man or woman earnestly seeking a grownup life ... will make the best of all the pupils in this age of clatter and buzz, of gape and gloat.

1953 *WSC to Florence Horsbrugh, Minister for Education 1951–4. The Trades Union Congress received Churchill's permission to reproduce the letter, which appeared in their 1953 Annual Report, pp. 173–4.*

Collective ideologists

... collective ideologists (those professional intellectuals who revel in decimals and polysyllables) ...

1953

Correctitude

... while observing every form of official correctitude he sought ruthlessly 'the way out'.

1931 *A favourite 19th-century word, 'correctitude' appears a dozen times in Churchill's writings: a combination of 'correct' and 'rectitude'.*

Cottonopolis

[We are] dependent absolutely for the maintenance of that marvellous structure of Lancashire industry, which is the wonder of the world and which has located Cottonopolis here in this unexpected spot; dependent absolutely upon the free imports of food and raw material.

1909

Disappearage

No, but perhaps a *disappearage* ...

1953 *To his son-in-law Christopher Soames, who suggested that Sir Harry Mackeson, a Conservative MP, should be relieved as Secretary for Overseas Trade, but did not deserve a peerage.*

Drinkable address

44 Avenue de Champagne is the world's most drinkable address.

1947 *Declared to Odette Pol-Roger concerning the address of his favourite producer of bubbly, Pol Roger Champagne.*

Drizzle of empires

A drizzle of empires, falling through the air.

1918 *Churchill to Eddie Marsh, after the surrender of Turkey on 29 October 1918. 'It was yesterday that Turkey gave in,' Marsh had written, 'and it will be Austria tomorrow.'*

Dull, drilled, docile

I see also the dull, drilled, docile, brutish masses of the Hun soldiery plodding on like a swarm of crawling locusts.

1941 *Superb alliteration was a memorable part of this famous speech on the German invasion of Russia.*

Earthly palimpsest

The trenches criss-cross one another; the monuments of dead commanders and shot-torn regiments are of different years. An earthly palimpsest of tragedy!

1929 *A palimpsest is a manuscript written over a partially obscured older manuscript in such a way that the original writing can still be read under the newer writing.*

Epileptic corpse

He is no better than an epileptic corpse.

1936 *Berating Baldwin for failing to tell the truth about German rearmament.*

Fearthought

Fearthought is futile worrying over what cannot be averted or will probably never happen.

1937

Female llama

A female llama who has been surprised in her bath.

1959 *Lady Limerick asked WSC if he had said this about de Gaulle. Lord Moran believed he did.*

Glittering pall

Over the landscape, brilliant with sunshine, snow had spread a glittering pall.

1906

Glittering scum

Cultured people are merely the glittering scum which floats upon the deep river of production.

1929 *Churchill's son Randolph had remarked that the oil magnates of Alberta were too uncultured to know how to spend their money properly.*

Gospeller

Like Henry VIII, [Arthur Balfour] decapitated Papists and burned hot Gospellers on the same day for their respective divergences in opposite directions from his central, personal and artificial compromise.

1923

Great state of affairs

Come in, come in, but tell me of no great affairs of State. There are none. There is only a great state of affairs.

1951

Improvose and dore

WSC to his naval aide: I sent him a signal – 'Improvise and dare' … He improvose and dore.

1943 *Reference to General Sir Henry Maitland ('Jumbo') Wilson, Commander-in-Chief Middle East, who had defended with few troops the Greek island of Leros.*

Je vous liquiderai. Si vous m'obstaclerez, je vous liquiderai!

1943 *While 'liquider' is a genuine French word, there is no verb 'obstaclerer'; WSC again makes a verb out of a noun. This is de Gaulle's version (Kersaudy); Harold Nicolson quoted it in proper French but I believe de Gaulle's is more authentic.*

Klop

When I say 'Klop', Miss Shearburn, that is what I want. [At other times:] Gimme klop!

WSC had an aversion to staples and paper clips, and preferred his documents to be klopped (hole-punched), then joined by a treasury tag. When an earlier secretary, Kathleen Hill, was first asked for 'klop', she proudly produced the 15-volume Der Fall des Hauses Stuart *by the German historian Onno Klopp (1822–1903). 'Christ almighty!' WSC roared.*

Lay an egg

I've been living on the Second World War. Now I shall live on this history [of the English-speaking peoples]. I shall lay an egg a year – a volume every twelve months should not mean much work.

1953 *'Now in my business, "laying an egg" has a rather different connotation,' said actor Robert Hardy in an address to the Churchill Centre, San Francisco, 1991.*

Lion-hearted limpets

Mr Attlee combines a limited outlook with strong qualities of resistance. He now resumes the direction and leadership of that cluster of lion-hearted limpets … who are united by their desire to hold on to office at all costs to their own reputations and their country's fortunes …

1951 *Prime Minister Attlee had returned to parliament from a brief hospitalisation.*

Luloo and Juloo

I was looking for a luloo, and who d'you think I ran into? Juloo.

Mary Soames to Laurence Olivier, who had been surprised in his dressing room at an intermission in a performance of Shaw's Caesar and Cleopatra. 'Oh, I'm sorry,' said Churchill, 'I was looking for a corner.' Olivier, playing Julius Caesar, had directed him to the loo.

Make hell while the sun shines

… it may be that the Japanese, whose game is what I may call 'to make hell while the sun shines', are more likely to occupy themselves in … seizing island bases for defensive purposes …

1942

Microphone and murder

These men [Mussolini and Hitler] of the microphone and murder …

1936

Mock-turtle soup

This contest is between 'the turtle soup of Tory Imperialism and the mock-turtle soup of Liberal Imperialism'.

1900

Mouth to hand

I earned my livelihood [in the 1930s] by dictating articles which had a wide circulation not only in Great Britain and the United States, but also, before Hitler's shadow fell upon them, in the most famous newspapers of sixteen European countries. I lived in fact from mouth to hand.

1948 *Churchill loved to turn common expressions on their ends.*

Mush, Slush and Gush

The cause of disarmament will not be attained by Mush, Slush and Gush.

1932

Namsosed

We shall need skis for that [landing again on the coast of Norway] and we don't want to go and get Namsosed again. We've had enough of that.

1940 *WSC refers to the outcome of operations where the enemy have control over the air, such as at Namsos, Norway, north of Trondheim, where the British were thrown back in April 1940.*

Naval holiday

Before the war I proposed to [head of the German navy, Admiral] von Tirpitz a naval holiday. If this had been accepted, it would enormously have eased the European tension, and possibly have averted the catastrophe.

1937 *In 1911 WSC had proposed a temporary stoppage in German and British new battleship construction.*

Nettle and dock

In looking at the views of these two Hon. Members I have always marvelled at the economy of nature which had contrived to grow from a single stock the nettle and the dock.

1905 *Edgar Vincent, First Viscount D'Abernon (1857–1941), Conservative MP 1899–1906, was a diplomat. His brother, Sir Charles Edward Howard Vincent (1849–1908), Conservative MP 1885–1908, was a soldier.*

Nickel lining

And now the British housewife, as she stands in the queue to buy her bread ration, will fumble in her pocket in vain for a silver sixpence. Under the Socialist Government nickel will have to be good enough for her. In future we shall be able to say: 'Every cloud has a nickel lining.'

1946 *On the Labour government's decision to mint sixpence coins made of nickel.*

Non-undisincentive

We should call it a non-undisincentive.

1950 *Stafford Cripps, then Chancellor of the Exchequer, had called the purchase tax a 'disincentive'. When a Tory MP said he thought the tax was not a fiscal weapon, WSC interjected his own description of it.*

Non-undisinflation

The word 'disinflation' has been coined in order to avoid the unpopular term 'deflation' … I suppose that when presently 'disinflation' also wins its bad name, the Chancellor [Sir Stafford Cripps] will call it 'non-undisinflation' and will start again.

1949

Order of the Boot

How can I accept the Order of the Garter, when the people of England have just given me the Order of the Boot?

1945 *WSC declining the Garter from King George VI, following the 1945 election.*

Paintatious

This is a most paintatious place!

Used throughout his years as a painter (1915–58) to describe beautiful, sunny places where he might paint continuously.

Porcupine eating

[Invading Burma from the north is like] eating the porcupine quill by quill.

1944

Pox Britannica

1907 *On his African journey, Churchill was informed by a colonial governor of the alarming spread of venereal disease among the native population.*

Prince Palsy

... I wanted to form a Balkan front. I wanted Yugoslavia, and I hoped for Turkey. That, with Greece, would have given us fifty divisions. A nut for the Germans to crack. Our intervention in Greece caused the revolution in Yugoslavia which drove out Prince 'Palsy'; and delayed the German invasion of Russia by six weeks. Vital weeks. So it was worth it. If you back a winner it doesn't really matter much what your reasons were at the time.

1948 *Prince Paul of Yugoslavia (1893–1976), regent of Yugoslavia for King Peter II from 1934 until he signed a pact with Nazi Germany in March 1941. Historians now believe this didn't delay the invasion of Russia.*

Pumpkin and Pippin

WSC: Have you spoken to Pumpkin?

Fitzroy Maclean: Pumpkin, Prime Minister? I'm afraid I don't understand what you mean.

WSC: Why, that great big general of mine. And what have you done with Pippin? [Maclean was at a loss.] Good God, they haven't got the code! Shall we scramble?

1944 *Fitzroy Maclean with WSC on radio telephone. 'Pumpkin' was WSC's portly General Maitland Wilson; 'Pippin' was his son Randolph, who was fighting with Maclean and the Yugoslav partisans. Invited to use the scrambler, Fitzroy replied that he thought he* was *scrambled.*

Purblind worldlings

... there are thoughtless dilettanti or purblind worldlings who sometimes ask us: 'What is it that Britain and France are fighting for?' To this I answer: 'If we left off fighting you would soon find out.'

1940

Queuetopia

Why should queues become a permanent, continuous feature of our life? Here you see clearly what is in their minds. The Socialist dream is no longer Utopia but Queuetopia. And if they have the power this part of their dream will certainly come true.

1950

Quisling

Indomitable patriots take different paths; quislings and collaborationists of all kinds abound; guerrilla leaders, each with their personal followers, quarrel and fight.

1944 *Vidkun Quisling (1887–1945), Norwegian army officer and fascist politician, Minister-President of occupied Norway 1942–5, was executed for treason at the end of the war. Churchill associated the use of his name as a synonym for 'traitor'.*

Re-rat

Anyone can rat, but it takes a certain amount of ingenuity to re-rat.

Churchill was referring to his desertion of the Conservatives for the Liberals in 1904, and his becoming a Conservative again officially in 1925.

Siren suit

Most sensible suit I ever had. Did you know that I designed it myself? You notice I have one extra large breast pocket. That's to hold my cigars.

1940s–1950s *'Siren suit' was WSC's term for what some staff called his 'rompers'. Originally of workaday fabrics, they grew increasingly luxurious as WSC warmed to them, and he would sometimes appear in them for dinner or similar occasions.*

Slatternly

Whatever one may think about democratic government, it is just as well to have practical experience of its rough and slatternly foundations.

1929 *A mid-17th-century word meaning 'slovenly'.*

Sofari so goody!

1907 *Coined during his African journey of late 1907. 'Safari' is Swahili for 'journey'.*

Soft underbelly

The soft underbelly of Europe …

In August 1942 in Moscow, WSC drew for Stalin a sketch of a crocodile, saying, 'We should rip open the soft underbelly in the Mediterranean.' Later he often he used 'soft underbelly' to describe the strategy of an attack from the south.

Some chicken; some neck

When I warned them [the French Government] that Britain would fight on alone whatever they did, their generals told their Prime Minister and his divided Cabinet, 'In three weeks England will have her neck wrung like a chicken.' Some chicken; some neck.

1941 *'Neck' as used here means impudence, cheek or chutzpah, as in 'brass neck'.*

Spurlos versenkt

I have searched the benches opposite with my eyes, but I cannot see any sign of the burly and engaging form of the Rt. Hon. Gentleman. He has departed *spurlos versenkt,* as the German expression says – sunk without leaving a trace behind.

1946 *Referring to the resignation of Mr Ben Smith, Minister of Food in the post-war Labour government.*

Squalid nuisance

Unless The Rt. Hon. Gentleman changes his policy and methods ... he will be as great a curse to this country in time of peace as he was a squalid nuisance in time of war.

1945 *A dripping sarcasm about his political enemy, Aneurin Bevan.*

'Stop the Home Fires Burning'

I must write to Novello and tell him to produce a good war song – but this time it will have to be 'Stop the Home Fires Burning'.

1940 *WSC to Sir John Slessor, musing on the relative dearth of World War II songs compared to World War I. Ivor Novello composed 'Keep the Home Fires Burning' during World War I.*

Stricken field

The Emir [Ahmed Fedil] had faithfully discharged his duty, and he was hurrying to his master's assistance with a strong and well-disciplined force of not less than 8,000 men when, while yet sixty miles from the city, he received the news of 'the stricken field'.

1899 *First occurrence of a favourite phrase. WSC may have read it in Scott or Macaulay. John McCrae's poem, 'The Unconquered Dead' was likely influential, since Churchill used 'stricken field' on at least four later occasions.*

Summer jewellery

... the garden gleams with summer jewellery. We live v[er]y simply – but with all the essentials of life well understood & well provided for – hot baths, cold champagne, new peas, & old brandy.

1915 *WSC to his brother Jack. He was on holiday at Hoe Farm, Godalming, Surrey, where he brooded over his dismissal from the Admiralty, and learned to paint. Like many of his generation who wrote letters in longhand, WSC used contractions 'vy, wh, yr' for 'very, which, your'.*

Suñer or later

Lady Churchill: I hope this was not wrong diplomatically.

WSC: Well, we will know Suñer or later!

1954 *Lady Churchill forwarded a request from the Spanish Foreign Minister, Suñer (pronounced 'Soon-yaire'), thought to have been pro-Nazi, who had asked her to help place his niece in an English convent.*

Tattered flag

Wise words, Sir, stand the test of time, and I am very glad the House has allowed me, after an interval of fifteen years, to raise the tattered flag I found lying on a stricken field.

1901 *Churchill's second speech in the House of Commons was a bravura performance. The 'tattered flag' was his father Lord Randolph's call, fifteen years earlier, for more economy in the budget. See 'Stricken field' above.*

Terminological inexactitude

The conditions of the Transvaal Ordinance under which Chinese labour is now being carried on do not, in my opinion, constitute a state of slavery. A labour contract … may not be a healthy or proper contract, but it cannot in the opinion of His Majesty's Government be classified as slavery in the extreme acceptance of the word without some risk of terminological inexactitude.

1906 *Churchill was disavowing that 'Chinese slavery' was in effect being practised in the Transvaal. Randolph Churchill wrote: 'This celebrated example of polysyllabic humour was always to be misunderstood and to be regarded as a nice substitute for "lie", which it plainly was not intended to be.'*

Thirteen feet of minister

I must press you to go to the Ministry of Transport … surely you must see that I cannot waste thirteen feet of Minister in a single department?

1952 *Lennox-Boyd stood six feet six inches tall, and his Secretary of State at the Colonial Office, Oliver Lyttelton, was scarcely shorter.*

Toil, blood, death, squalor

War today is bare – bare of profit and stripped of all its glamour. The old pomp and circumstance are gone. War now is nothing but toil, blood, death, squalor, and lying propaganda.

1932

Triphibian

He [Lord Louis Mountbatten] is what … I will venture to call 'a complete triphibian'.

1943 *'Triphibious' (capable of living or operating on land, water and air) entered the* Oxford English Dictionary *in 1986. Its first appearance was by Leslie Hore-Belisha in* The Times *of 4 November 1941, but 'triphibian' is traced to a news article in the* Baltimore Sun *of 26 October 1935.*

Ungrateful volcano

We are paying eight millions a year for the privilege of living on an ungrateful volcano out of which we are in no circumstances to get anything worth having.

1922 *Unsent letter to Lloyd George, referring to Iraq.*

Unregulated unthinkability

It is only a little while ago that I heard ministers say, and read diplomatic documents which said, that rearmament was unthinkable – 'Whatever happens, we cannot have that. Rearmament is unthinkable.' Now all our hope is to regulate the unthinkable. Regulated unthinkability – that is the proposal now; and very soon it will be a question of making up our minds to unregulated unthinkability.

1934

Unsordid

[President Roosevelt] devised the extraordinary measure of assistance called Lend-Lease, which will stand forth as the most unselfish and unsordid financial act of any country in all history.

1945 *This word to describe Lend-Lease was first coined by Churchill on 10 November 1941. Often incorrectly believed to have been said about the post-war Marshall Plan.*

Wincing Marquess

Lord Lansdowne has explained, to the amusement of the nation, that he claimed no right on behalf of the House of Lords to mince the Budget. All, he tells us, he has asked for, so far as he is concerned, is the right to wince when swallowing it. Well, that is a much more modest claim. It is for the Conservative Party to judge, whether it is a very heroic claim for one of their leaders to make. If they are satisfied with the wincing Marquess, we have no reason to protest.

1909

Winstonian

It is very kind of you to write me such a long letter. It will be carefully preserved among the Winstonian archives.

1905 *When no word was available, WSC would coin his own. As the years passed, his contemporaries used 'Winstonian' to describe Churchill's friends and causes – not always in the positive sense.*

Woomany

You will let me come up for a week to see you and Woomany I am sure.

1888 *Winston's name for his beloved nanny, Elizabeth Everest, a word that seemed to combine thoughts like 'woman and home', which she forever represented to him.*

Wormwood Scrubbery

The Socialist ideal is to reduce us to one vast Wormwood Scrubbery.

1946 *Wormwood Scrubs is a prison in West London.*

Wounded canary

I am not going to tumble around my cage like a wounded canary. You knocked me off my perch. You have now got to put me back on my perch. Otherwise I won't sing.

1944 *On a clause in the Education Bill which threatened the government*

with losing a vote of confidence. 'Everybody was ruffled and annoyed,'
wrote Harold Nicolson. 'The only person who really enjoyed it was
Winston himself. He grinned all over.'

Wuthering Height

Thank God we have seen the last of that Wuthering Height!

circa **1940** *Said of a 'tall lugubrious colleague', according to Colin Brooks,*
editor of the Sunday Dispatch, *1936–8. Most sources agree that he was Sir*
John Reith, who as BBC director had kept Churchill off the air during
WSC's Wilderness Years, but who was later made Minister of Transport and
then Minister of Works in the wartime coalition. Wuthering Heights, *Emily*
Brontë's only novel, was published in 1847.

5. Great communicator

Churchill's skills as a wordsmith and orator are pervasive throughout his work, but the following show his love of language and the principles that made him the greatest communicator of his time. Included are his advice about English, book and speech composition, dating, dictation, style and usage.

Churchill crisply dismissed faddish expressions and jargon: we can guess what he would say about modern abominations like 'chairperson'. With foreign languages, he saw no reason to patronise foreigners by overemphasising their pronunciation. In fact, purposely Anglicised words did not appeal to him. He frowned on name changes – like Iran for Persia or Ankara for Angora – and studiously mispronounced the Uruguayan capital as 'Monty-viddy-oh'. Perhaps he didn't notice when China went from Peiping to Peking to Beijing, but we have a fair idea what he would think about it.

Book composition
I write a book the way they built the Canadian Pacific Railway. First I lay the track from coast to coast, and then I put in all the stations.

circa 1946

Books: his own
To sit at one's table on a sunny morning, with four clear hours of uninterruptible security, plenty of nice white paper, and a Squeezer pen [laughter] – that is true happiness.

1908[1] *A 'Squeezer' was the then-new fountain pen, refilled by dipping the nib in ink and squeezing a bladder.*

Field-Marshal Smuts: Oh, Winston, why? Why did you have to do that? You, more than anybody in the world, could have written as no one else could have written, the true history of the war, and instead of that you have produced these books.

WSC: This is *my* story. If someone else likes to write *his* story, let him.

late 1940s[2] *This story may have gained a little in the telling, writes David Dilks, Lord Tedder's research assistant for his book, who heard him relate it in various forms.*

Writing a book is an adventure. To begin with it is a toy, then an amusement. Then it becomes a mistress, and then it becomes a master, and then it becomes a tyrant and, in the last stage, just as you are about to be reconciled to your servitude, you kill the monster and fling him to the public.

1949[3] *Other versions of this quotation are incorrect or incomplete. That above is from the original speaking notes. I have made one correction, which WSC no doubt made when he spoke: the draft notes read 'became a mistress'.*

... already in 1900, which is a long time ago, I could boast to have written as many books as Moses, and I have not stopped writing them since, except when momentarily interrupted by war, in all the intervening period.

1950[4] *The 'five books of Moses' were Genesis, Exodus, Leviticus, Numbers and Deuteronomy.*

Breadth of a comma
I am glad that we have found a common ground to stand on, though it be only the breadth of a comma.
1910

Brevity
Pray inform me on one sheet of paper ...
1940s[1]

Is it really necessary to describe the [German battleship] *Tirpitz* as the *Admiral von Tirpitz* in every signal? This must cause a

considerable waste of time for signal men, cipher staff and typists. Surely *Tirpitz* is good enough for the beast.
1942[2]

This Treasury paper, by its very length, defends itself against the risk of being read.
circa 1940s[3] *WSC quoted by Norman Brook.*

Chartwell factory

Do come and see my factory. This is my factory. This is my secretary ... And to think I once commanded the fleet.
1930s *Recalled with a smile by his long-time secretary, Grace Hamblin, who knew he said this to tease her.*

Classical literature

... as a schoolboy I questioned the aptness of the Classics for the prime structure of our education. So they told me how Mr Gladstone read Homer for fun, which I thought served him right ...
1930

'Consultation'

... one can always consult a man and ask him, 'Would you like your head cut off tomorrow?' and after he has said, 'I would rather not,' cut it off. 'Consultation' is a vague and elastic term.
1947

Curate's egg

However we may regard Sir Stafford Cripps's record there is no doubt he has shouldered the main weight of the Government's task. He has a brain, which, at any rate, is something to begin with. He has also a conscience which, like the curate's egg, is good in parts.
1948 *The curate's egg stemmed from an 1895* Punch *cartoon. Served a bad egg, the young curate told his host the bishop: 'Oh no, my Lord, I assure you, parts of it are excellent.'*

Dictation

My dear, I shall require you to stay extremely late. I am feeling very fertile tonight.

1930s[1] WSC to a secretary coming on duty. Another version: 'I am feeling very fertile; I shall require two young women tonight.'

Oh dear, she's very young. I mustn't frighten her! ... Don't worry if you don't get it all – I always remember what I've said.

1930s[2] The first part of this quotation is WSC to his wife; the second to a new, 19-year-old secretary on her first dictation.

Drafts

Your task, my boy, is to make Cosmos out of Chaos.

1947[1] WSC to literary assistant Denis Kelly, who set about organising the messy Chartwell muniment room.

The fact that I did not use [your draft] in no way detracts from the help you gave me. It gave me a rope with which to crawl ashore till I could walk on my own feet up the beach.

1950[2] To George Christ, Parliamentary Liaison Officer, Conservative Central Office. Although his name was pronounced to rhyme with 'wrist', Churchill liked to shout: 'Send for Christ!'

English

We have history, law, philosophy and literature; we have sentiment and common interest; we have a language which even the Scottish Nationalists will not mind me referring to as English.

1954

Facts vs rumour

The chronicler of ill-recorded times has none the less to tell his tale. If facts are lacking, rumour must serve. Failing affidavits, he must build with gossip.

1933

Foreign names and pronunciation

The news which has come from Montevideo ['Monty-viddy-oh'] has been received with thankfulness … The pocket battleship *Graf Speee* [long emphasis on the 'e's'] … has met her doom.

1939[1]

Jack, when you cross Europe you land at Marsay, spend a night in Lee-on and another in Par-ee, and, crossing by Callay, eventually reach Londres. I land at Marsales, spend a night in Lions, and another in Paris, and come home to LONDON!

circa 1940[2] *WSC to his friend Jack Seely, later Lord Mottistone.*

Don't be so BBC – the place is WALLSHAVEN!

circa 1940[3] *When Captain Pim, who ran WSC's map room, pronounced Walshaven as 'Varls-harvern'.*

I always thought it was a most unfortunate and most tiresome thing when both Persia and Mesopotamia changed their names at about the same time to two names which were so much alike – Iran and Iraq. I have endeavoured myself in the domestic sphere to avoid such risks [in naming ministers].

1941[4]

I refuse to call it El Alamein. Like those asses who talk about Le Havre. *Harver* the place is to any decent man. Now this third battle must be called 'The Battle of Egypt'. Harold, see to that at once. Tell your people henceforward to call it The Battle of Egypt.

1942[5] *WSC to General Alexander. Churchill did use 'Alamein' but refused to countenance 'El'.*

Sebastapol's good enough for me, young man.

1945[6] *After the Yalta conference he was told by a Russian-speaking RAF officer that arrangements had been made to fly him home via 'Sevastapol'.*

... Constantinople should never be abandoned, though for stupid people Istanbul may be written in brackets after it. As for Angora, long familiar with us through the Angora cats, I will resist to the utmost of my power its degradation to Ankara ... Fortune is rightly malignant to those who break with the traditions and customs of the past. As long as I have a word to say in the matter Ankara is banned, unless in brackets afterwards. If we do not make a stand we shall in a few weeks be asked to call Leghorn Livorno, and the BBC will be pronouncing Paris 'Paree'. Foreign names were made for Englishmen, not Englishmen for foreign names. I date this minute from St George's Day.

1945[7]

'Grand Remonstrance'

... my father set out to examine me [on history]. The period was Charles I. He asked me about the Grand Remonstrance; what did I know about that? I said that in the end the Parliament beat the King and cut his head off. This seemed to me the grandest remonstrance imaginable.

1930

History

History with its flickering lamp stumbles along the trail of the past, trying to reconstruct its scenes, to revive its echoes, and kindle with pale gleams the passion of former days.

1940

Hyphens and 'e's'

I am in revolt about your hyphens. One must regard the hyphen as a blemish to be avoided wherever possible. Where a composite word is used it is inevitable, but ... [my] feeling is that you may run them together or leave them apart, except when nature revolts ... 'Judgment' no 'e'. If so there would have to be 'abridgement' and why not 'developement'?

Whereas I always write 'development'. The Oxford Dictionary gives it as optional and I am very much inclined to opt.

1934 *WSC to his long-time secretary and literary assistant, Eddie Marsh.*

Jargon

This grimace is a good example of how official jargon can be used to destroy any kind of human contact or even thought itself.

1951 *Reference was to Soviet Foreign Minister Molotov's woolly 1942 memo: '[We] will be in a position to draw the necessary conclusions as to the real state of affairs, particularly in regard to certain irregularities in the actions of the respective British naval authorities.'*

Language

I have no objection to a proper use of strong language, but a certain amount of art and a certain amount of selective power is needed, if the effect is to be produced.

1925[1]

We all remember how Queen Elizabeth dealt with poetry and blank verse – 'Marry, this is something. This is rhyme! But this' – the blank verse – 'is neither rhyme nor reason.'

1948[2]

Latin

The foreigners and the Scotch have joined together to introduce a pronunciation of Latin which divorces it finally from the English tongue ... They have distorted one of my most serviceable and impressive quotations into the ridiculous booby 'Wainy, Weedy, Weeky'. Punishment should be reserved for those who have spread this evil.

1930[1] *Since Churchill rarely used 'Scotch' for 'Scots', we may assume that he did so here on purpose.*

WSC: I must now warn the House that I am going to make an unusual departure. I am going to make a Latin quotation. It is one which I hope will not offend the detachment of the old school tie and will not baffle or be taken as a slight upon the new spelling brigade. Perhaps I ought to say the 'new spelling squad' because it is an easier word. The quotation is '*Arma virumque cano*', which, for the benefit of our Winchester friends, I may translate as 'Arms and the men I sing'. That generally describes my theme.

Mr Hugh Gaitskell (Labour): Should it not be 'man', the singular instead of the plural?

WSC: Little did I expect that I should receive assistance on a classical matter from such a quarter. I am using the word 'man' in a collective form which, I think, puts me right in grammar.

1953[2]

Leave the past to history

For my part, I consider that it will be found much better by all Parties to leave the past to history, especially as I propose to write that history myself.

1948

Maiden speech

It is difficult to avoid the conclusion that the moderation of the Amendment was the moderation of the Hon. Member's [Lloyd George's] political friends and leaders, and that the bitterness of his speech is all his own.

1901[1] *Often misquoted, including by Churchill himself in* My Early Life.

… Mr Bowles whispered 'You might say "instead of making his violent speech without moving his moderate amendment, he had better have moved his moderate amendment without making his violent speech".' Manna in the wilderness was not more welcome! … I was up before I knew it, and reciting Tommy Bowles's rescuing sentence. It won a general cheer … Everyone

was very kind. The usual restoratives were applied, and I sat in a comfortable coma till I was strong enough to go home.
1930[2]

Man vs woman

WSC: ... just the ordinary man who keeps a wife and family, who goes off to fight for his country when it is in trouble, goes to the poll at the appropriate time, and puts his cross on the ballot paper showing the candidate he wishes to be elected to Parliament ... he is the foundation of democracy. And it is also essential to this foundation that this man ...

Dr Edith Summerskill (Labour): And woman.

WSC: I beg pardon. There is always the stock answer that man *embraces* woman, unless the contrary appears in the context.
1944

Mein Kampf as a Koran

All was there – the programme of German resurrection; the technique of party propaganda; the plan for combating Marxism; the concept of a National-Socialist State; the rightful position of Germany at the summit of the world. Here was the new Koran of faith and war: turgid, verbose, shapeless, but pregnant with its message.
1948

Melting

The Government stock is very low. They are like a great iceberg which has drifted into warm seas and whose base is being swiftly melted away, so that it must topple over.
1935

Newspapers (media)

We live in the most thoughtless of ages. Every day headlines and short views.
1929[1]

Fancy cutting down those beautiful trees we saw this afternoon to make pulp for those bloody newspapers, and calling it civilisation.

1929[2]

These gentlemen of the press were listening carefully to every word you said – all eagerly anxious for a tiny morsel of cheese which they could publish. And you go and give them a whole ruddy Stilton!

1941[3] *Rebuke to a general who had spoken too openly about an upcoming attack on Benghazi in North Africa.*

No comment ... I think 'no comment' is a splendid expression. I am using it again and again. I got it from Sumner Welles during his tour of Europe.

1946[4] *As he was leaving for Miami before his seminal 'Iron Curtain' speech, reporters asked what he was going to speak about, and whether it involved the Russians. Sumner Welles (1892–1961) was Under-Secretary of State for President Roosevelt, 1936–43.*

Nobel Prize for Literature
I am proud, but also I must admit, awestruck at your decision to include me. I do hope you are right. I feel we are both running a considerable risk and that I do not deserve it. But I shall have no misgivings if you have none.

1953

Novel *Savrola*
I have consistently urged my friends to abstain from reading it.

1930[1]

Emerson said, 'Never read any book that is not a year old.' I can at least give reassurance on this point, since *Savrola* first appeared in print in *Macmillan's Magazine* in 1897 [1899] when I was twenty-three. The preface to the first edition in 1900 [1899] submitted the book 'with considerable trepidation to the judgement or the clemency of the public'. The intervening fifty-five years have somewhat dulled though certainly not changed my sentiments on this point.

1956[2] *WSC was wrong on the dates;* Savrola *was serialised from May to December 1899 and the American edition appeared before 1900.*

Oratory

If you have an important point to make, don't try to be subtle or clever. Use a pile driver. Hit the point once. Then come back and hit it again. Then hit it a third time.

1919[1] *Advice to the Prince of Wales, later Edward VIII.*

One must not yield too easily to the weaknesses of audiences. There they were; what could they do? They had asked for it, and they must have it.

1930[2] *Reflecting on his first political speech, to the Primrose League at Claverton Manor (now the American Museum), Bath, 1897.*

Improvised be damned! I thought of it this morning in my bath and I wish now I hadn't wasted it on this crowd.

1932[3] *Harold Nicolson asked if he had improvised a phrase extemporaneously.*

I wasn't talking to you, Norman, I was addressing the House of Commons.

undated[4] *WSC to his valet, Norman MacGowan, who rushed into WSC's bathroom after hearing 'ominous mutterings'.*

Originality

Those Greeks and Romans, they are so overrated. I have said just as good things myself. They owe their reputation to the fact that they got in first with everything.

undated

'Outwith'

I must thank the Hon. Gentleman for making me acquainted
with the word 'outwith', with which I had not previously had
the pleasure of making acquaintance. For the benefit of English
Members I may say that it is translated 'outside the scope of'.
I thought it was a misprint at first.

1944

'Piebald'

I well appreciate the necessity of preserving the piebald
complexion of my pony.

1941 *On balancing the parties in his precarious wartime coalition.*

'Piles and water'

The Venetian Republic would have perished in a moment if the
waters of the Mediterranean had ever broken down the
supports on which the city was raised above them; and the life
of Egypt was bound up with the inundation of the Nile. And
the Venetians were always thinking about their piles, and the
Egyptians were always thinking about their water.

1908

Poetry: 'Puggy-wug'

Oh, what is the matter with poor Puggy-wug?
Pet him and kiss him and give him a hug.
Run and fetch him a suitable drug,
Wrap him up tenderly all in a rug,
That is the way to cure Puggy-wug.

1930s *WSC's youngest daughter Mary had a pug who became ill. 'My
father was greatly upset at our distress,' wrote her sister Sarah, 'and
although he really thought that poetry, though enjoyable, was a minor sort
of thing – prose being much more important – he composed this ditty for
Mary and me … which we all chanted while Puggy was ill.'*

Poetry: 'The Influenza'

Oh how shall I its deeds recount
Or measure the untold amount
Of ills that it has done?
From China's bright celestial land
E'en to Arabia's thirsty sand
It journeyed with the sun.

O'er miles of bleak Siberia's plains
Where Russian exiles toil in chains
It moved with noiseless tread;
And as it slowly glided by
There followed it across the sky
The spirits of the dead.

The Ural peaks by it were scaled
And every bar and barrier failed
To turn it from its way;
Slowly and surely on it came,
Heralded by its awful fame,
Increasing day by day.

On Moscow's fair and famous town
Where fell the first Napoleon's crown
It made a direful swoop;
The rich, the poor, the high, the low
Alike the various symptoms know,
Alike before it droop.

Nor adverse winds, nor floods of rain
Might stay the thrice-accursed bane;
And with unsparing hand,
Impartial, cruel and severe
It travelled on allied with fear
And smote the fatherland.

Fair Alsace and forlorn Lorraine,
The cause of bitterness and pain
In many a Gallic breast,
Receive the vile, insatiate scourge,
And from their towns with it emerge
And never stay nor rest.

And now Europa groans aloud,
And 'neath the heavy thunder-cloud
Hushed is both song and dance;
The germs of illness wend their way
To westward each succeeding day
And enter merry France.

Fair land of Gaul, thy patriots brave
Who fear not death and scorn the grave
Cannot this foe oppose,
Whose loathsome hand and cruel sting,
Whose poisonous breath and blighted wing
Full well thy cities know.

In Calais port the illness stays,
As did the French in former days,
To threaten Freedom's isle;
But now no Nelson could o'erthrow
This cruel, unconquerable foe,
Nor save us from its guile.

Yet Father Neptune strove right well
To moderate this plague of Hell,
And thwart it in its course;
And though it passed the streak of brine
And penetrated this thin line,
It came with broken force.

For though it ravaged far and wide
Both village, town and countryside,
Its power to kill was o'er;
And with the favouring winds of Spring
(Blest is the time of which I sing)
It left our native shore.

God shield our Empire from the might
Of war or famine, plague or blight
And all the power of Hell,
And keep it ever in the hands
Of those who fought 'gainst other lands,
Who fought and conquered well.

1890 *Churchill's longest poem, included for its literary qualities.*

Political correctness

I hope you have all mastered the official Socialist jargon
which our masters, as they call themselves, wish us to learn.
You must not use the word 'poor'; they are described as the
'lower income group'. When it comes to a question of
freezing a workman's wages the Chancellor of the Exchequer
speaks of 'arresting increases in personal income'. The idea is
that formerly income taxpayers used to be the well-to-do, and
that therefore it will be popular and safe to hit at them. Sir
Stafford Cripps does not like to mention the word 'wages',
but that is what he means. There is a lovely one about houses
and homes. They are in future to be called 'accommodation
units'. I don't know how we are to sing our old song 'Home
Sweet Home'. 'Accommodation Unit, Sweet Accommodation
Unit, there's no place like our Accommodation Unit.' I hope
to live to see the British democracy spit all this rubbish from
their lips.

1950

Pot-boilers

Why will people keep referring to that bloody pot-boiler?

1961 *Remark when his private secretary sent a copy of* Thoughts and Adventures, *containing his essay 'Moses', to David Ben-Gurion. Secretary Grace Hamblin reported: 'potboilers', as he called them [were] articles for magazines or the national newspapers on topical subjects … very exciting because they were done in one evening, quickly put out and sent off usually the next day. He got his money very quickly, which he liked too. We all liked doing potboilers.*

'Prefabricated'

… we must have a better word than 'prefabricated' [for houses]. Why not 'ready-made'?

1944 *WSC to Minister of Works.*

Punctuation

WSC: You are very free with your commas. I always reduce them to a minimum: and use 'and' or an 'or' as a substitute not as an addition. Let us argue it out.

Eddie Marsh: I look on myself as a bitter enemy of superfluous commas, and I think I could make a good case for any I have put in – but I won't do it any more!

WSC: No do continue. I am adopting provisionally. But I want to argue with you.

1922[1]

In the art of drafting [income tax law] there seems to be a complete disdain of the full stop, and even the humble colon is an object to be avoided.

1927[2]

'Quantify'… 'short supply'

I was shocked to hear [Sir Stafford Cripps use the word 'quantify']. I hope he never uses it again … Another expression that is very common today is, 'in short supply'. Why can't you say 'scarce'? Then there is 'broken down'.

All that means is 'sifting', or if you wish to be more erudite, you say 'analyse'.

1940s Churchill was a powerful advocate of compactness and the avoidance of flowery substitutes for ordinary words. One can only imagine what he would say about the modern practice of making verbs out of nouns: 'We will effort that today.'

Quotations

It is a good thing for an uneducated man to read books of quotations ... The quotations when engraved upon the memory give you good thoughts.

1930[1]

I am reminded of the professor who, in his declining hours, was asked by his devoted pupils for his final counsel. He replied, 'Verify your quotations.'

1951[2]

Reading

Young people, I believe, should be careful in their reading, as old people in eating their food. They should not eat too much. They should chew it well.

1934

'Screened'

That is a curious phrase [screened] which has crept in. 'Sifted' would have been a more natural word ... 'Screened' is a modern vulgarism.

1947

Shakespeare

My Lord Hamlet, may I use your lavatory?

1950s WSC to Richard Burton in Burton's dressing room, after Churchill had sat in a front row, speaking the lines of Hamlet *with him.*

'Snafu'

Yes, it should have been; indeed it was our intention to do it. It is only as the result of what in the United States is known as a 'snafu' – which word I have added to my vocabulary – that you were not consulted about it.

1952 A member of parliament had asked why Britain wasn't consulted about Korean bombing operations. 'Snafu' means 'situation normal: all fouled up'. Sometimes another f-word is substituted.

'Stand firm'

Neither is the expression 'Stay Put' really applicable to the districts where fighting is going on. First of all, it is American slang; secondly, it does not express the fact. The people have not been 'put' anywhere. What is the matter with 'Stand Fast' or 'Stand Firm'? Of the two I prefer the latter. This is an English expression and it says exactly what is meant …
1941

Style

Broadly speaking, short words are best and the old words when short are best of all.
1949[1]

Personally, I like short words and vulgar fractions.
1953[2]

'Trepanning'

I am told that there is good evidence to show that the system of dealing with time-bombs by trepanning is proving very successful … Will you please let me have a report on the extent to which trepanning is being used.

1940 'Trepanning' was an ancient practice of opening the skull to operate on the brain, or to remove a core from a cylindrical object. Apparently WSC was the first to apply the word to defusing bombs.

'Unilateral'

If the bride or bridegroom fails to turn up at church, the result is not what, to use an overworked word, is called a 'unilateral' wedding. The absolute essence of the matter is that both parties should be there.

1946

Usage

… you distinguish in several cases between enemy aircraft 'out of action' or 'destroyed'. Is there any real difference between the two, or is it simply to avoid tautology? If so, this is not in accordance with the best authorities on English. Sense should not be sacrificed to sound.

1940[1] *Prime Minister to Secretary of State for Air.*

We 'invade' all countries with whom we are at war. We 'enter' all subjugated Allied lands we wish to 'liberate'. With regard to a country like Italy, with whose Government we have signed an armistice, we 'invaded' in the first instance, but, in view of the Italian cooperation, we must consider all further advances by us in Italy to be in the nature of 'liberation'.

1944[2]

6. People

The idea that Churchill cared nothing for other people, frequently inferred by his critics, resounds oddly to students of his words. In reviewing what Churchill said about people, what we mainly find in the end is understanding and magnanimity, but culling out his wittier remarks about people may very well tend to present the picture of a Churchill who preferred to make fun of others. The wisecracks about Neville Chamberlain reprinted herein are not a balanced account of Churchill's regard for Chamberlain, which he maintained through the worst of their disagreements, ending in his magnificent valedictory following Chamberlain's death in November 1940: 'The only guide to a man is his conscience ...'

So let it be said at the outset that the following witticisms are only a partial indication of his views of the persons named – chosen only for their wit and humour.

Asquith, Margot

Margot was a great woman, impudent, audacious, a flaming creature. Asquith counted it his greatest achievement when he pulled down this glittering bird on the wing. Besides, she took him into a world different from the bourgeois world he had known, and that counted for something in those days.

1944 *Margot Asquith (1864–1945), socialite and wit, wife of H. H. Asquith (Prime Minister, 1908–16).*

Astor, Nancy

I feel you have come into my bathroom and I have only a sponge with which to defend myself.

1919 *Nancy Witcher Astor, Viscountess Astor CH (1879–1964), the first woman to take a seat in Parliament, was MP for Plymouth Sutton, 1919–45. Lady Astor had said that when she first entered the Commons (1 December 1919), Churchill was very cold to her and she had asked him why.*

Attlee, Clement

Get up, get up, Lord Privy Seal! This is no time for levity.

1940[1] *Clement Richard Attlee (1883–1967), Labour MP, Deputy Prime Minister in the wartime coalition, Labour Prime Minister 1945–51. Attlee had fallen over his seat in the Commons chamber.*

Like the grub that feeds on the Royal Jelly and thinks it's a Queen Bee.

1946[2]

He has much to be modest about.

1946[3]

Baldwin, Stanley

[Mr Baldwin] is still quite a distinguished painter in our academy. If I were to criticise him at all I would say his work lacked a little in colour, and was also a little lacking in the precise definition of objects in the foreground. He too has changed not only his style but also his subjects … Making a fair criticism, I must admit there is something very reposeful about the half-tones of Mr Baldwin's studies.

1932[1] *Stanley Baldwin, first Earl Baldwin of Bewdley (1867–1947), Conservative MP and three times Prime Minister (1923–4, 1924–9, 1935–7).*

In those days the Lord President was wiser than he is now; he used frequently to take my advice.

1935[2]

Occasionally he stumbled over the truth, but hastily picked himself up and hurried on as if nothing had happened.

1936[3]

Baldwin was a remarkable man. I like to make people do what I wish. Baldwin liked to do what they wanted. But he was a great party organiser.

1952[4]

Balfour, Arthur

That old grey tabby is going to abolish the Naval Division.

1916 *Arthur James Balfour, first Earl of Balfour (1848–1930), Prime Minister 1902–5.*

Beaverbrook, Lord

Some people take drugs; I take Max.

circa 1941 *William Maxwell Aitken, first Baron Beaverbrook (1879–1964), Anglo-Canadian press owner and politician, WSC's first Minister of Aircraft Production.*

Beresford, Lord Charles

He is one of those orators of whom it was well said, 'Before they get up, they do not know what they are going to say; when they are speaking, they do not know what they are saying; and when they sit down, they do not know what they have said.'

1912 *Charles William de la Poer Beresford, first Baron Beresford (1846–1919), British Admiral and MP.*

Bevan, Aneurin

I should think it was hardly possible to state the opposite of the truth with more precision.

1944[1] *Aneurin ('Nye') Bevan (1897–1960), Welsh Labour MP, founder of the National Health Service.*

We speak of the Minister of Health, but ought we not rather to say Minister of Disease, for is not morbid hatred a form of mental disease, and indeed a highly infectious form? Indeed, I can think of no better step to signalise the inauguration of the National Health Service than that a person who so obviously needs psychiatrical attention should be among the first of its patients.

1948[2]

I was, I think, the first in this House to suggest, in November 1949, recognition of the Chinese Communists ... if you recognise anyone it does not necessarily mean that you like him. We all, for instance, recognise the Rt. Hon. Gentleman, the Member for Ebbw Vale.

1952[3]

Bonar Law, Andrew

How is our ambitious invalid? What about our gilded tradesman?

1922[1] *Andrew Bonar Law (1858–1923), Conservative MP, Prime Minister 1922–3.*

You dance like a will-o'-the-wisp so nimbly from one unstable foothold to another that my plodding paces can scarcely follow you ...

circa 1922[2]

Bossom, Alfred

Bossom, Bossom, that's an odd name! Neither one thing nor the other.

undated *Alfred Bossom, Baron Bossom (1881–1965), a popular Conservative known for his lavish receptions.*

Bryan, William Jennings

What Bryan has done is like an inebriate regulating a chronometer with a crowbar.

1896 *William Jennings Bryan (1860–1925), American politician, three-time Democratic nominee for President.*

Buller, Redvers

He plodded on from blunder to blunder and from one disaster to another, without losing either the regard of his country or the trust of his troops, to whose feeding as well as his own he paid serious attention.

1930 *General Sir Redvers Henry Buller (1839–1908), British general active in the Boer War.*

Butler, R. A.

He is always patting himself on the back, a kind of exercise that no doubt contributes to his excellent condition.

1954 *Richard Austen Butler, Baron Butler of Saffron Walden (1902–1982), Conservative MP, known as 'Rab', Chancellor of the Exchequer 1951–5 and mooted, but twice passed over, for the premiership.*

Cecil, Lord Hugh

Here for the first time, and I am afraid almost for the last, I met a real Tory, a being out of the seventeenth century, but equipped with every modern convenience and aptitude.

1931 *Hugh Richard Heathcote Cecil, First Baron Quickswood (1869–1956), Conservative MP 1895–1906 and 1910–37, best man at WSC's wedding.*

Chamberlain, Austen

… he donned an orchid regardless of expense and screwed on an eyeglass regardless of discomfort.

1907[1] *Sir Joseph Austen Chamberlain (1863–1937), Conservative MP 1892–1937, son of Joseph Chamberlain and half-brother of Neville.*

Austen always played the game – and always lost it.

1945[2]

Chamberlain, Joseph

Mr Chamberlain loves the working man, he loves to see him work!

1905[1] *Joseph Chamberlain (1836–1914), the great Liberal statesman, an early mentor to young Churchill, split with WSC over Free Trade (he favoured protective tariffs); he was leader of Liberal Unionists in Parliament and the father of Austen and Neville Chamberlain.*

His fiercest opponents would welcome his re-entry into the political arena … instead of the melancholy marionettes whom the wire-pullers of the Tariff Reform League are accustomed to exhibit on provincial platforms.

1909[2]

Chamberlain, Neville

What is the point in crying out for the moon when you have the sun, when you have the bright orb of day in whose refulgent beams all the lesser luminaries hide their radiance?

1938[1] *Arthur Neville Chamberlain (1869–1940), Prime Minister 1937–40.*

It doesn't matter where you put it [the podium], as long as he has the sun in his eyes and the wind in his teeth.

1939[2] *Churchill to his long-time friend Molly, Duchess of Buccleuch, who informed him that Chamberlain was coming to address the local Conservatives.*

History with its flickering lamp stumbles along the trail of the past, trying to reconstruct its scenes, to revive its echoes, and kindle with pale gleams the passion of former days. What is the worth of all this? The only guide to a man is his conscience; the only shield to his memory is the rectitude and sincerity of his actions ... we do ourselves and our country honour in saluting the memory of one whom Disraeli would have called an 'English worthy'.

1940[3]

... that was not an insuperable task, since I admired many of Neville's great qualities. But I pray to God in his infinite mercy that I shall not have to deliver a similar oration on Baldwin. That indeed would be difficult to do.

1940[4]

Chaplin, Charlie

He is a marvellous comedian – bolshy in politics and delightful in conversation.

1929 *Sir Charles Spencer Chaplin (1889–1977), English comedy actor and Hollywood film star.*

Churchill, Lady Randolph

The wine of life was in her veins. Sorrows and storms were conquered by her nature and on the whole it was a life of sunshine.

1921 *WSC to Lord Curzon on the death of his mother.*

Churchill, Winston (American novelist)

Mr Winston Churchill presents his compliments to Mr Winston Churchill, and begs to draw his attention to a matter which concerns them both ... Mr Winston Churchill has decided to sign all published articles, stories, or other work 'Winston Spencer Churchill' and not 'Winston Churchill' as formerly ... He takes this occasion of complimenting Mr Winston Churchill upon the style and success of his works, which are always brought to his notice whether in magazine or book form, and he trusts that Mr Winston Churchill has derived equal pleasure from any work of his that may have attracted his attention.

1899[1] *Winston Churchill the novelist (1871–1947) replied: 'Mr Winston Churchill is extremely grateful to Mr Winston Churchill for bringing forward a subject which has given Mr Winston Churchill much anxiety'.*

Why don't you go into politics? I mean to be Prime Minister of England: it would be a great lark if you were President of the United States at the same time.

1900[2] *American Winston won election to the New Hampshire Legislature (1903, 1905) but rose no higher, being defeated in a run for governor on the Bull Moose ticket in 1912.*

Cripps, Stafford

He is a lunatic in a country of lunatics, and it would be a pity to move him.

1940[1] *The Hon. Sir Richard Stafford Cripps (1889–1952), Labour MP, ambassador to Russia in World War II, Chancellor of the Exchequer in the post-war Labour government.*

… there is a man who habitually takes his meal of a handful of peas, and, when he gets a handful of beans, counts that his Christmas feast!

1943[2]

Neither of his colleagues can compare with him in that acuteness and energy of mind with which he devotes himself to so many topics injurious to the strength and welfare of the State.

1946[3]

Cromwell, Oliver

I understood definitely that he had blown up all sorts of things and was therefore a very great man.

1930 *Oliver Cromwell (1599–1658) was Lord Protector of Republican England from 1653 until his death.*

Crossman, R. H. S.

The Hon. Member is never lucky in the coincidence of his facts with the truth.

1954 *Richard Howard Stafford Crossman (1907–74), Labour MP and editor of the* New Statesman.

Curzon, George

The morning had been golden; the noontide was bronze; and the evening lead. But all were solid, and each was polished till it shone after its fashion.

1929 *The Hon. George Nathaniel Curzon, first Marquess Curzon of Kedleston KG GCSI GCIE PC (1859–1925), Viceroy of India and Conservative Foreign Secretary.*

Dalton, Hugh

The Hon. Gentleman is trying to win distinction by rudeness.

1926[1] *Edward Hugh John Neale Dalton, Baron Dalton (1887–1962), Labour MP, 1922–51, Chancellor of the Exchequer, 1945–7.*

Dr Dalton, the practitioner who never cured anyone, in his 'rake's progress' at the Exchequer, spent in his Budgets for three years over £10,000,000,000.

1948[2]

de Gaulle, Charles

I am no more enamoured of him than you [Roosevelt] are but I would rather have him on the committee than strutting about as a combination Joan of Arc and Clemenceau.

1943[1] *Charles André Joseph Marie de Gaulle (1890–1970), French general, Free French leader in WWII, President of the Fifth Republic (1958–69).*

I brought him up from a pup, but I never got him properly trained to the house.

1943[2]

de Valera, Eamon

No sooner had he clambered from the arena into the Imperial box, than he hastened to turn his thumb down upon the first prostrate gladiator he saw.

1938[1] *Eamon de Valera (1882–1975). Served Ireland as President and Premier, among other offices, between 1917 and 1973. In 1938 he urged recognition of the Italian conquest of Abyssinia.*

I understand that his view – a characteristically Irish view – is that the only way to unite the two islands is to dissolve every possible connection between them.

1938[2]

Dulles, John Foster

I will have no more to do with Dulles, whose great slab of a face I dislike and distrust.

1953[1] *Reconstructed from Colville's third-person rendition in his diaries. John Foster Dulles (1888–1959), US Secretary of State under Eisenhower 1953–59, took a hard line against new approaches to the Russians.*

Dull–duller–Dulles.

circa 1953[2] *Listed as unattributed in* Churchill by Himself.

This fellow preaches like a Methodist Minister, and his bloody text is always the same ... Ten years ago I could have dealt with him. Even as it is I have not been defeated by this bastard. I have been humiliated by my own decay.

1953[3]

Mr Dulles makes a speech every day; has a press conference every other day; and preaches on Sundays. All this tends to rob his utterances of real significance.

circa 1954[4]

He is the only case of a bull I know who carries his china closet with him.

1954[5] *Not positively verified, and misquoted by Manchester (1983, 34). Represented only as 'ear witness' by Kay Halle.*

Halifax, Earl

... he is one of those Christians who ought to be thrown to the lions.

1931 *Edward F. L. Wood, first Earl of Halifax, earlier Lord Irwin (1881–1959), Viceroy of India 1926–31, Foreign Secretary 1938–40, Ambassador to the United States 1941–46. In 1931, a devout Anglo-Catholic, the then-Lord Irwin successfully proposed a Round-Table conference on Indian self-government, producing this exclamation from WSC.*

Hearst, William Randolph

... a grave simple child – with no doubt a hasty temper – playing with the most costly toys. A vast income always overspent: ceaseless building and collecting not very discriminatingly works of art: two magnificent establishments, two charming wives; complete indifference to public opinion, a strong liberal and democratic outlook, a 15 million daily circulation, oriental hospitalities, extreme personal courtesy

(to us at any rate), the appearance of a Quaker elder – or perhaps Mormon elder.
1929

Hitler, Adolf
The gent has taken off his clothes and put on his bathing-suit, but the water is getting colder and there is an autumn nip in the air.

1940[1] *WSC to Roosevelt about Hitler's preparations to invade Britain. Adolf Hitler (1889–1945) German Chancellor 1933–45 and Nazi Party leader.*

Hitler forgot about this Russian winter. He must have been very loosely educated. We all heard about it at school; but he forgot it. I have never made such a bad mistake as that.
1942[2]

I always hate to compare Napoleon with Hitler, as it seems an insult to the great Emperor and warrior to connect him in any way with a squalid caucus boss and butcher.
1943[3]

When Herr Hitler escaped his bomb on July 20th he described his survival as providential; I think that from a purely military point of view we can all agree with him, for certainly it would be most unfortunate if the Allies were to be deprived, in the closing phases of the struggle, of that form of warlike genius by which Corporal Schicklgruber has so notably contributed to our victory.
1944[4]

Hopkins, Harry
Sancho P. [= Sancho Panza = Harry Hopkins] was looking extraordinarily well, and twice as fit as he was before the combined restoratives of blood transfusions and matrimony were administered to him.

1943 *WSC to his wife. Harry Lloyd Hopkins (1890–1946), Roosevelt's personal envoy to Britain and Russia and Special Assistant to the President. WSC nicknamed him after Don Quixote's faithful squire.*

Inönü, Ismet

Do you know what happened to me today, the Turkish President kissed me. The truth is I'm irresistible. But don't tell Anthony [Eden], he's jealous.

1943 *WSC to his daughter Sarah. Mustafa Ismet Inönü (1884–1973), second President of Turkey, 1938–50.*

Joynson-Hicks, William

The worst that can be said about him is that he runs the risk of being most humorous when he wishes to be most serious.

1931 *William Joynson-Hicks, first Viscount Brentford, known as 'Jix', (1865–1932), Conservative MP.*

King Edward VII

… I am curious to know about the King. Will it entirely revolutionise his way of life? Will he sell his horses and scatter his Jews or will Reuben Sassoon be enshrined among the crown jewels and other regalia? Will he become desperately serious? Will he continue to be friendly to you? Will the Keppel be appointed the 1st Lady of the Bedchamber? Write to tell me all about all this.

1901 *WSC to his mother. Albert Edward (1841–1910), King of Great Britain and Ireland and Emperor of India, 1901–10. Alice Keppel was his most famous mistress.*

King Ibn Saud

I was the host and I said that if it was his religion that made him say such things, my religion prescribed as an absolute sacred ritual smoking cigars and drinking alcohol before, after, and if need be during, all meals and the intervals between them. Complete surrender.

1945 *Abdul Aziz ibn Saud (1876–1953) had declared that his religion forbade smoking and drinking alcohol.*

Kinna, Patrick

It's no use throwing you out. There's not enough of you to make a ham sandwich.

circa **1944** *Patrick Kinna (1913–2009) was a wartime Churchill secretary present at many summit conferences. They were returning from the European continent in a Dakota which suddenly began losing power and altitude, and the crew contemplated what to jettison to lighten the payload.*

Kitchener, Field Marshal Lord

He had disapproved of me severely in my youth, had endeavoured to prevent me from coming to the Soudan Campaign, and was indignant that I had succeeded in getting there. It was a case of dislike before first sight.

1923 *Horatio Herbert Kitchener, First Earl Kitchener of Khartoum (1850–1916).*

Lenin, Vladimir

Lenin was sent into Russia by the Germans in the same way that you might send a phial containing a culture of typhoid or cholera to be poured into the water supply of a great city, and it worked with amazing accuracy.

1919[1] *Vladimir Ilyich Ulyanov, alias Lenin (1870–1924), Russian revolutionary, first head of the Russian Soviet Federated Socialist Republic (1917–22).*

His sympathies cold and wide as the Arctic Ocean; his hatreds tight as the hangman's noose. His purpose to save the world: his method to blow it up ... He alone could have led Russia into the enchanted quagmire; he alone could have found the way back to the causeway. He saw; he turned; he perished ... The Russian people were left floundering in the bog. Their worst misfortune was his birth; their next worst – his death.

1929[2]

Lloyd George, David

At his best he could almost talk a bird out of a tree.

1931 *First Earl Lloyd-George of Dwyfor (1863–1945), Welsh MP, Liberal Prime Minister 1916–22.*

MacDonald, Ramsay

We know that he has, more than any other man, the gift of compressing the largest number of words into the smallest amount of thought …

1933 *James Ramsay MacDonald (1866–1937), first Labour Prime Minister, 1924; formed his second government in 1929; coalition Prime Minister 1931–5.*

Maclean, Fitzroy

Here is the young man who has made a Public Convenience of the Mother of Parliaments.

1942 *WSC to Jan Smuts, introducing Fitzroy Maclean, who had got himself out of the Foreign Office and into the army by standing for Parliament. Sir Fitzroy Hew Royle Maclean of Dunconnel KT (1911–1996), diplomat, writer and politician.*

Malenkov, Georgy

Sir Robert Menzies on the resignation of Malenkov: I expect he has gone to Siberia.

WSC: Oh no, more likely he has gone to join Beria.

1955 *Georgy Maximillianovich Malenkov (1902–1988), Premier of the Soviet Union following the death of Stalin, 6 March 1953 to 8 February 1955. Lavrenti Beria, chief of the Soviet secret police, was executed by order of his own colleagues shortly after Stalin's death.*

McCarthy, Senator Joseph

He's spoiling a good cause.

1950s *Joseph Raymond McCarthy (1908–1957), US Senator from Wisconsin 1947–57, famous for overstated claims about communists in the US government.*

Monro, General Sir Charles

General Monro was an officer of swift decision. He came, he saw, he capitulated.

1923 Charles Carmichael Monro (1860–1929) replaced Ian Hamilton as Commander of British Forces at Gallipoli, October 1915, and supervised the evacuation.

Moran, Lord

... we divide our labours; he instructs me in the art of public speaking, and I teach him how to cure pneumonia.

1944 Charles McMoran Wilson, First Baron Moran (1882–1977), Churchill's personal physician 1940–65.

Mountbatten, Lord Louis

Have you no sense of glory? What could you do if you returned to sea, except to be sunk in a larger and more expensive vessel?

1941 Admiral of the Fleet the Earl Mountbatten of Burma (1900–79). WSC to Mountbatten after the latter expressed reluctance to become Chief of Combined Operations. Mountbatten's destroyer, HMS Kelly, had been sunk under him on 23 May 1941.

Mussolini, Benito

This whipped jackal, Mussolini, who to save his own skin has made all Italy a vassal state of Hitler's Empire, comes frisking up at the side of the German tiger with yelpings not only of appetite – that can be understood – but even of triumph ... this absurd impostor will be abandoned to public justice and universal scorn.

1941 Benito Amilcare Andrea Mussolini (1883–1945), Prime Minister and dictator of Italy 1922–43.

Peake, Osbert

Peake hates old people (as such) living too long and cast a critical eye on me ... I felt v[er]y guilty. But in rejoinder I took him in to my study and showed him the 4 packets of proofs of the History of the E.S. Peoples wh[ich] bring 50,000 dollars a year into the island on my account alone. 'You don't keep me. I keep you.' He was rather taken aback.

1954 *Osbert Peake, later first Viscount Ingleby (1897–1966), Minister of Pensions and National Insurance in the Churchill government during 1954–5.*

Pick, Frank

Shake him by the hand! Shake him by the hand! You can say to St Peter that you have met the perfect man … If I am stricken down by enemy action, I hope that, when I appear before my Maker, it will serve me in good stead to have been so recently in the company of a man without sin.

1941[1] *Frank Pick (1878–1941), Chairman of the London Passenger Transport Board, 1933–40, had rejected publishing a clandestine newspaper to subvert the enemy, on ethical grounds.*

Never let me see that–that–that canting bus driver again.

1941[2] *WSC wrote this (in red ink) after hearing that Pick had been relieved of his post.*

Plasteras, Nikolaos

I know nothing of this Plasterarse. I do trust he will not prove to have feet of clay.

1945 *As with so many foreign words, WSC's pronunciation of the name was literal. General Nikolaos Plastiras (1883–1953) was Greek Prime Minister in 1945, 1950 and 1951–52.*

Pound, Admiral Sir Dudley

Dudley Pound's a funny old boy. People think he's always asleep, but you've only got to suggest reducing the naval estimates by a million and he's awake in a flash.

1941[1] *Admiral of the Fleet Sir Alfred Dudley Pickman Rogers Pound (1877–1943), First Sea Lord 1939–43.*

His face was set. He could not speak. But he took my hand, and when I said things that might be agreeable to him, he gripped it hard. His mind was all right; he knew what I was saying. He died on Trafalgar Day. Death is the greatest gift God has made to us.

1943[2]

Reves, Wendy

Daisy, Wendy is three things you will never be. She is young, she is beautiful, and she is kind.

circa 1959 *Wendy Russell Reves (1916–2007), wife of Churchill's literary agent Emery Reves and his frequent hostess in the south of France. Remark to socialite Daisy Fellowes.*

Savinkov, Boris

He was that extraordinary product – a Terrorist for moderate aims. A reasonable and enlightened policy – the Parliamentary system of England ... freedom, toleration and good will – to be achieved wherever necessary by dynamite at the risk of death.

1929[1] *Boris Victorovich Savinkov (1879–1925), Vice Minister of War in the 1917 Kerensky Government, ousted by Lenin's Bolsheviks in November 1917.*

He was the essence of good sense expressed in terms of nitroglycerine.

1919[2]

Shinwell, Emanuel

I do not challenge the Hon. Gentleman when the truth leaks out of him by accident from time to time.

1944[1] *Emanuel Shinwell, Baron Shinwell (1884–1986) Labour MP 1922–67. He often sparred with Churchill across the floor, but they had a mutual affection.*

I should, of course, treat with great attention anything he might say upon the subject of contradictory statements by politicians or Ministers. He is a past master of the art himself.
1952[2]

I must have been too complimentary to the Rt. Hon. Gentleman. He has explained what harm any compliment from me did to him, I must really rake up a few more compliments.
1953[3]

Smuts, Jan Christian

Smuts and I are like two old love-birds moulting together on a perch, but still able to peck.

circa **1944–5** *Jan Christian Smuts (1870–1950) was twice Prime Minister of South Africa (1919–24, 1939–48). One of Churchill's closest friends from the Boer War forward.*

Snowden, Philip

A perverse destiny has seemed to brood over the Rt. Hon. Gentleman's career; all his life has been one long struggle to overcome the natural amiability of his character.

1925[1] *Philip Snowden, First Viscount Snowden (1864–1937), Labour MP and first Labour Chancellor of the Exchequer (1924); Churchill thought highly of him.*

The Treasury mind and the Snowden mind embraced each other with the fervour of two long-separated kindred lizards, and the reign of joy began ... He was a preaching friar with no Superior to obey but his intellect ...
1931[2]

Spee, Admiral Maximilian von

To steam at full speed or at high speed for any length of time on any quest was to use up his life rapidly. He was a cut flower in a vase; fair to see, yet bound to die, and to die very soon if the water was not constantly renewed.

1923 *Maximilian Graf von Spee (1861–1914) commanded the German East Asia Squadron from 1912.*

Stalin, Josef

WSC: The first two hours were bleak and sombre ... Then I spoke of the bombing of Germany, and he seemed a little more friendly. I thought that was the time to produce TORCH. Stalin was at last listening with both his ears. 'May God prosper this undertaking,' he said.

Lord Moran: Did he really say that?

WSC: Oh, he brings in the Deity quite a lot.

1942[1] *After returning from his first meeting with Stalin, where WSC said there would be no 'Second Front' in Europe in 1942; TORCH was the invasion of North Africa.*

WSC: England is becoming a shade pinker.

Stalin: That is a sign of good health. I want to call Mr Churchill my friend.

WSC: Call me Winston. I call you Joe behind your back.

Stalin: No, I want to call you my friend. I'd like to be allowed to call you my good friend.

1943[2]

Silly tales have been told of how these Soviet dinners became drinking-bouts. There is no truth whatever in this. The Marshal and his colleagues invariably drank their toasts from tiny glasses, taking only a sip on each occasion. I had been well brought up ... [Then Stalin said,] 'You are leaving at daybreak. Why should we not go to my house and have some drinks?' I said that I was in principle always in favour of such a policy.

1950[3] *Josef Vissarionovich Dzhugashvilli, later Stalin (1878–1953), General Secretary of the Soviet Communist Party Central Committee, 1922–53.*

Trotsky, Leon

... a skin of malice stranded for a time on the shores of the Black Sea and now washed up in the Gulf of Mexico. He possessed in his nature all the qualities requisite for the art of civic destruction – the organising command of a Carnot, the cold detached intelligence of a Machiavelli, the mob oratory of a Cleon, the ferocity of a Jack the Ripper, the toughness of Titus Oates ...

1929 *Leon Trotsky (Lev Davidovich Bronstein, 1877–1940), communist leader after Lenin's death; defeated by Stalin, 1924, for control of the Communist Party, exiled to Mexico and later killed by Soviet agents.*

Truman, Harry

At any rate, he is a man of immense determination. He takes no notice of delicate ground, he just plants his foot down firmly upon it.

1945 *Harry S. Truman (1884–1972), 33rd President of the United States (1945–53). To make his point, Churchill gave a little hop, smacking his bare feet on the floor.*

Webb, Beatrice

I refuse to be shut up in a soup-kitchen with Mrs Sidney Webb.

1908 *When WSC turned down the presidency of the local government board. Martha Beatrice Potter Webb (1858–1943), socialist reformer.*

Welldon, Bishop

It was from [my] slender indications of scholarship that Mr Welldon drew the conclusion that I was worthy to pass into Harrow. It is very much to his credit. It showed that he was a man capable of looking beneath the surface of things: a man not dependent upon paper manifestations. I have always had the greatest regard for him.

1930 *James Edward Cowell Welldon (1854–1937), Head Master of Harrow 1885–8, later Bishop of Calcutta.*

Wilson, Woodrow

The spacious philanthropy which he exhaled upon Europe
stopped quite sharply at the coasts of his own country.

1929 *Thomas Woodrow Wilson (1856–1924), 28th President of the United
States, 1912–20.*

Wodehouse, P. G.

Let him go to hell – as soon as there's a vacant passage.

1944 *Sir Pelham Grenville Wodehouse (1881–1975), English comic writer,
who injudiciously made broadcasts to America over German radio.*

7. Britain, Empire and Commonwealth

In the age of 'deconstruction' (as they call lying about history), we often hear: 'Yes, Churchill was indispensable in 1940, but remember that his supreme motivation was British interests.' The better-read would suggest that of course Churchill upheld British interests; but in harmony with the interests of others, notably the United States. And it's obvious that not being overrun by Hitler's Germany was the prime British interest in Churchill's supreme hour.

The argument that Churchill hastened the demise of the Empire can be similarly discounted. The Empire's days were numbered with the emergence of independent Dominions, the Irish Treaty and the Government of India Act in the first third of the 20th century. Most British leaders understood that, and hoped that Empire would lead to Commonwealth and an interdependent 'British Community'. If that didn't work out, it was the fault of many other than Churchill.

Churchill believed that British parliamentary government was the least imperfect form of democracy which 'could save and guide the world'. Readers interested in the full panoply of his wit and wisdom on Britain and the Empire-Commonwealth should refer to relevant chapters in *Churchill by Himself*.

Achievements
If it be true, as has been said, that every country gets the form of government it deserves, we may certainly flatter ourselves.
1945

Classes
We have had a leisured class. It has vanished. Now we must think of the leisured masses.
1953

Climate

... the British people have always been superior to the British climate. They have shown themselves capable of rising above it ...

1948

Commonwealth of Nations

For some years the tendency of Socialist and Left-Wing forces has been to gird at the word 'Empire' and espouse the word 'Commonwealth', because Oliver Cromwell cut off King Charles's head and all that. Also, I suppose, because the word 'Commonwealth' seems to have in it some association with, or suggestion of, the abolition of private property and the communal ownership of all forms of wealth.

1948

Criticism, Churchill's

... I see little glory in an Empire which can rule the waves and is unable to flush its sewers.

1901 *In 1908, the Liberal MP Charles Masterman cynically remarked: 'Winston is full of the poor, whom he has just discovered.'*

Defence

Our country should suggest to the mind of a potential paratrooper the back of a hedgehog rather than the paunch of a rabbit.

1951

Empire defined

... the British Empire existed on the principles of a family and not on those of a syndicate.

1907

Empire rioting

Indeed a terrible position. An angry mob, armed with staves and stones, inflamed by alcohol, and inspired by Liberal principles!

1952 *After an account of rioting in Bechuanaland.*

Empire's end

I have not become the King's First Minister in order to preside over the liquidation of the British Empire. For that task, if ever it were prescribed, someone else would have to be found ...

1942[1]

I am a bit sceptical about universal suffrage for the Hottentots even if refined by proportional representation. The British and American Democracies were slowly and painfully forged and even they are not perfect yet.

1954[2] *Eisenhower was unaware of British efforts to bring countries in Africa and Asia to independence; WSC tactfully explained this, while expressing his scepticism about the speed with which the efforts were proceeding.*

Englishmen and Arabs

The Arab was an African reproduction of the Englishman; the Englishman a superior and civilised developement [sic] of the Arab.

1899 *The older spelling of 'development' prevails throughout the first edition of* The River War.

Geography

Our island is surrounded by the sea. It always has been, and although the House may not realise it, the sea was in early times a great disadvantage because an invader could come across the sea and no one knew where he would land; very often he did not know himself.

1933

Gibraltar

The establishment of the apes on Gibraltar should be twenty-four and every effort should be made to reach this number as soon as possible and maintain it thereafter.

1944 WSC to Colonial Secretary. Legend has it that if the apes ever leave Gibraltar Britain's rule there will end. From Churchill's time the ape colony has thrived magnificently.

Humbug

I had no idea in those days of the enormous and unquestionably helpful part that humbug plays in the social life of great peoples.

1930

London

London, like a great rhinoceros, a great hippopotamus, saying: 'Let them do their worst. London can take it.'

1945[1]

I must congratulate you on having got a magnificent new roof over your heads and amid all the problems of housing for the people not to have left Gog and Magog out in the cold.

1954[2] Gog and Magog (named for nations of the earth deceived by Satan in Revelations XX: 7–9) were a pair of 1708 nine-foot statues at the Guildhall, destroyed in the Blitz; they were replaced by replicas.

Obligations

We are resolved to make this Island solvent, able to earn its living and pay its way … we have no assurance that anyone else is going to keep the British Lion as a pet.

1951

People

… a blunderbuss is a traditional weapon with which the British householder defends himself from those who seek to plunder him.

1901[1]

... the British public, and the great nation which inherits this somewhat foggy island, are less likely to be grateful for benefits received than they are for evils averted.

1927[2]

Golding, look at this: Improper advances ... below zero ... 76 years old ... Makes you proud to be an Englishman!

1946[3] *WSC read a news article that an elderly gentleman was arrested on a very cold evening in Hyde Park 'for making improper advances to a young lady'.*

People in war
The nose of the bulldog has been slanted backwards so that he can breathe without letting go.

1914[1]

The British people have taken for themselves this motto – 'Business carried on as usual during alterations on the map of Europe.'

1914[2]

The British people do not, as is sometimes thought, go to war for calculation, but for sentiment.

1945[3] *WSC to Marshal Stalin.*

Scotland
Now that I shall be commanding a Scottish battalion, I should like you to send me a copy in one volume of Burns. I will soothe and cheer their spirits by quotations from it. I shall have to be careful not to drop into a mimicry of their accent! You know I am a great admirer of that race. A wife, a constituency, and now a regiment attest the sincerity of my choice!

1916[1]

I have myself some ties with Scotland which are to me of great significance – ties precious and lasting. First of all, I decided to be born on St Andrew's Day – and it was to Scotland I went to find my wife, who is deeply grieved not to be here today through temporary indisposition. I commanded a Scottish battalion of the famous 21st Regiment for five months in the line in France in the last war. I sat for fifteen years as the representative of 'Bonnie Dundee', and I might be sitting for it still if the matter had rested entirely with me.

1942[2]

Uganda

Uganda is defended by its insects.

1908[1] *An inscription by WSC on a copy of his travel book,* My African Journey.

Fancy mistaking a hippopotamus – almost the largest surviving mammal in the world – for a water lily. Yet nothing is more easy.

1908[2]

Virgin Islands

[In a defence discussion a Cabinet minister said, 'I'm afraid I don't know where the Virgin Islands are. Do you, Prime Minister?'] Not exactly, but I trust they lie at a respectable distance from the Isle of Man.

1940s

Wales

Môr o gân yw Cymru i gyd [All Wales is a Sea of Song].

1951 *WSC had appointed Welshman David Llewellyn as an under-secretary to the Home Office charged with Welsh affairs, announcing, 'His name is quite well known throughout the Principality.' A Welsh MP shouted: 'Pronounce it.' 'I will,' said Churchill – 'Llewellyn.' Then he stunned the House with this phrase, which he had heard at an* Eisteddfod *(Welsh festival) thirty years before.*

8. Nations

Churchill admired the United States, but with qualification. Though his best-known public criticism was 'toilet paper too thin, newspapers too fat!' he had harsh words in private for certain U.S. institutions and leaders, but he never lost faith in America's destiny or capacity for good.

His view of Germany was a combination of admiration, concern, reproach and magnanimity, and sometimes all four at once. Yet he was the first to urge postwar rapprochement between France and Germany. He never warmed to Russia, and before World War II often referred to its leaders as Bolsheviks. After they joined the war he more often called them Russians. Yet after Russia acquired the atomic bomb, Churchill spent his waning years in office trying desperately to reach an understanding that would avoid a nuclear catastrophe.

Of former British possessions like Canada and India, Churchill never altered his view that Britain's colonial record had set the stage for the democracies they became. In 1922 he helped engineer an Irish Treaty that kept the peace there for nearly fifty years. Generally he admired small states that stood up for their rights – Greece, Yugoslavia, Denmark and Norway all contributed heroics despite cruel occupation. And he despised countries which allowed themselves to be subjugated without a struggle.

Australia

The silence of the bush and the loneliness of the desert are only disturbed by the passing of some transcontinental express, the whirr of a boomerang, or the drone of a pilotless missile.

1958

Canada

I have had a most successful meeting at Winnipeg. Fancy 20 years ago there were only a few mud huts – tents ... and last night a magnificent audience of men in evening dress & ladies half out of it ...

1901[1] *To his mother during his Canadian lecture tour.*

The French Canadians derived greater pleasure from singing 'God Save the King' than from singing 'Rule Britannia'.
1904[2]

Canada is the linchpin of the English-speaking world.
1941[3]

A very odd thing that when I woke up very early this morning, I thought what a pity I haven't got one of those lovely Canadian hats ... people often think I am hot-headed. It fits beautifully, and is large enough to allow for any swelling which may take place.

1941[4] *Churchill had been presented with a British Columbia seal wedge cap.*

... I have been all over Canada in my time and I have the most vivid pictures in my mind of many places from Halifax to Kicking Horse Valley and further on to Vancouver, where I caught a lovely salmon, a beautiful salmon, in the harbour in about twenty minutes. In fact I think one of the only important places that I have never visited in Canada is Fort Churchill ...
1954[5]

China

China, as the years pass, is being eaten by Japan like an artichoke, leaf by leaf.
1937[1]

There is another Chinese saying about their country which dates only from the fourth century: 'The tail of China is large and will not be wagged.' I like that one. The British democracy approves the principle of movable heads and unwaggable national tails.

1952[2]

Cuba

The most remarkable fact seems to be that two armies [Spain's and the Cuban rebels'] will shoot at each other for hours and no one will get hit. I believe that statisticians say that in a battle it takes 2,000 bullets to kill a man. When the calculations are arranged I think it will be found that in the Cuban war it took 2,000 bullets to miss each individual combatant.

1895

Czechoslovakia

Here was the model democratic State of Central Europe, a country where minorities were treated better than anywhere else. It has been deserted, destroyed and devoured. It is now being digested.

1938

Denmark

The Danish sailors from the 'long ships' who fought ashore as soldiers brought with them into England a new principle represented by a class, the peasant-yeoman proprietor ... the peculiar esteem in which law and freedom are held by the English-speaking peoples in every quarter of the globe may be shrewdly and justly referred to a Viking source.

1950

Egypt

... the Egyptian is not a fighting animal ... He may be cruel. He is never fierce. Yet he is not without courage ... It is the courage of down-trodden peoples, and one which stronger breeds may often envy, though they can scarcely be expected to admire.
1899[1]

The Khedive's attitude [to the British Agent] reminded me of a school-boy who is brought to see another school-boy in the presence of the headmaster. But he seemed to me to be an amiable young man who tries to take an intelligent interest in the affairs of his kingdom, which, since they have passed entirely beyond his control, is, to say the least of it, very praiseworthy.
1899[2]

... I could not bear his leaving without seeing the Sphinx ... We motored there ... Roosevelt and I gazed at her for some minutes in silence. She told us nothing and maintained her inscrutable smile. There was no use waiting longer.
1952[3]

France

The British are good at paying taxes, but detest drill. The French do not mind drill, but avoid taxes. Both nations can still fight, if they are convinced there is no other way of surviving; but in such a case France would have a small surplus and Britain a small army.
1937[1]

Frenchmen! For more than thirty years in peace and war I have marched with you. I am marching still along the same road ... Here at home in England, under the fire of the Boche, we do not forget the ties and links that unite us to France ... our Air Force has more than held its own. We are waiting for the long-promised invasion. So are the fishes.
1940[2]

The Almighty in His infinite wisdom did not see fit to create Frenchmen in the image of Englishmen.

1942[3]

I am going to give you a warning: be on your guard, because I am going to speak, or try to speak, in French, a formidable undertaking and one which will put great demands on your friendship for Great Britain.

1944[4]

Germany

… politics in Germany are not what they are over here. There you do not leave office to go into opposition. You do not leave the front bench to sit below the gangway. You may well leave your high office at a quarter of an hour's notice to drive to the police station, and you may be conducted thereafter, very rapidly, to an even harder ordeal.

1934[1]

Cabinet Minister: 'The trouble with the Germans is that they are like a lot of sheep; they will follow anybody.' Oh, it is far worse than that, they are *carnivorous* sheep!

1943[2]

The proud German Army has by its sudden collapse [in North Africa] proved the truth of the saying, 'The Hun is always either at your throat or your feet'; and that is a point which may have its bearing upon the future.

1943[3]

Greece

Hitler has told us that it was a crime in such circumstances on our part to go to the aid of the Greeks. I do not wish to enter into argument with experts.

1941[1]

The Greeks rival the Jews in being the most politically-minded race in the world … No two cities have counted more with mankind than Athens and Jerusalem.
1952[2]

India

The Sikh is the guardian of the marches. He was originally invented to combat the Pathan.
1898[1]

It makes me sick when I hear the Secretary of State saying of India, 'She will do this,' and 'she will do that.' India is an abstraction … India is no more a political personality than Europe. India is a geographical term. It is no more a united nation than the Equator.
1931[2]

Ireland

If Ireland were more prosperous she would be more loyal, and if more loyal more free.
1904[1]

Ireland is not a daughter State. She is a parent nation.
1921[2]

I remember on the eve of the Great War … we discussed the boundaries of Fermanagh and Tyrone. Both of the great political parties were at each other's throats. The air was full of talk of civil war … Then came the Great War … Every institution, almost, in the world was strained. Great Empires have been overturned. The whole map of Europe has been changed. The position of countries has been violently altered. The modes of thought of men, the whole outlook on affairs, the grouping of parties, all have encountered violent and tremendous changes in the deluge of the world, but as the

deluge subsides and the waters fall short, we see the dreary steeples of Fermanagh and Tyrone emerging once again. The integrity of their quarrel is one of the few institutions that has been unaltered in the cataclysm which has swept the world.
1922[3]

… in Ireland almost everything happens when you do not expect it, and anything which any large number of people expect never happens.
1922[4]

My nurse, Mrs Everest, was nervous about the Fenians. I gathered these were wicked people and there was no end to what they would do if they had their way. On one occasion when I was out riding on my donkey, we thought we saw a long dark procession of Fenians approaching. I am sure now it must have been the Rifle Brigade out for a route march. But we were all very much alarmed, particularly the donkey, who expressed his anxiety by kicking. I was thrown off and had concussion of the brain. This was my first introduction to Irish politics!
1930[5]

No one knows what they are. They are neither in nor out of the Empire. But they are much more friendly to us than they used to be. They have built up a cultured Roman Catholic system in the South. There has been no anarchy or confusion. The bitter past is fading.
1947[6]

Israel

But you ought to let the Jews have Jerusalem; it is they who made it famous.
1955 *WSC to Eden's private secretary Evelyn Shuckburgh.*

Italy

I have never known a case of a great athlete being a great general – no prize-fighter has ever been a good general. The only exception might be in the Italian Army, where a general might find it useful to be a good runner.

1941[1]

The hyena [Mussolini] in his nature broke all bounds of decency and even common-sense …

1942[2]

Japan

'Sir … In view of these wanton acts of unprovoked aggression, committed in flagrant violation of international law … His Majesty's Ambassador at Tokyo has been instructed to inform the Imperial Japanese Government in the name of His Majesty's Government in the United Kingdom that a state of war exists between our two countries. I have the honour to be, with high consideration, Sir, Your obedient servant, Winston S. Churchill.' Some people did not like this ceremonial style. But after all when you have to kill a man it costs nothing to be polite.

1941[1] *Mamoru Shigemitsu (1887–1957), Ambassador to Britain (1938–41), was paroled from a war sentence in 1950 and served as Foreign Minister in 1954–6.*

[Japan's leaders] have certainly embarked upon a very considerable undertaking. [Laughter] … What kind of a people do they think we are?

1941[2] *This line in WSC's first speech to Congress brought all to their feet, even previous isolationist senators and representatives cheering.*

Jordan

The Emir Abdullah is in Transjordania, where I put him one Sunday afternoon at Jerusalem.

1936

Morocco

[Marrakesh is] the Paris of the Sahara, where all the caravans had come from Central Africa for centuries to be heavily taxed en route by the tribes in the mountains and afterwards swindled in the Marrakesh markets, receiving the return, which they greatly valued, of the gay life of the city, including fortune-tellers, snake-charmers, masses of food and drink, and on the whole the largest and most elaborately organised brothels in the African continent. All these institutions were of long and ancient repute.

1950[1]

Everybody liked shoving their paws into the dish and remembered with pleasure that fingers were made before forks. The Glaoui is as old as I am but quite lively. He pretends to know neither French nor English, but I believe he understands everything that is said, at least in French ... The music brays and squawks and tom-toms, and the singing, which was maintained throughout, was a masterly compendium of discords ...

1950[2] *On a visit to El Hadji Thami El Glaoui, Pasha of Marrakesh and hereditary Sultan of the Atlas.*

Palestine

The Rt. Hon. and Learned Gentleman, the President of the Board of Trade [Sir Stafford Cripps] spoke of the past twenty-five years as being the most unkind or unhappy Palestine has known. I imagine that it would hardly be possible to state the opposite of the truth more compendiously ...

1946

Poland

It would be a great pity to stuff the Polish goose so full of German food that it died of indigestion.

1945 WSC to Stalin in reference to compensating Poland for losses of territory to the east by shifting her borders west into what had been German territory.

Russia

One might as well legalise sodomy as recognise the Bolsheviks.
1919[1]

After having defeated all the tigers and lions I don't like to be beaten by baboons.
1919[2]

… in Russia a man is called a reactionary if he objects to having his property stolen, and his wife and children murdered.
1919[3]

There is not one single social or economic principle or concept in the philosophy of the Russian Bolshevik which has not been realised, carried into action, and enshrined in immutable laws a million years ago by the White Ant.
1927[4]

Were [Britain, France and America in 1919] at war with Soviet Russia? Certainly not … It was, they repeated, a matter of indifference to them how Russians settled their own internal affairs. They were impartial – Bang!
1929[5]

All sorts of Russians made the revolution. No sort of Russian reaped its profit.
1931[6]

I cannot forecast to you the action of Russia. It is a riddle wrapped in a mystery inside an enigma: but perhaps there is a key. That key is Russian national interest.
1939[7]

Everybody has always underrated the Russians. They keep their own secrets alike from foe and friends.
1942[8]

His father's ghost: 'Is there still a Tsar?'

WSC: Yes, but he is not a Romanoff. It's another family.

1947[9]

... the day will come when it will be recognised without doubt ... that the strangling of Bolshevism at its birth would have been an untold blessing to the human race.

1949[10]

South Africa

....the Boer is a curious combination of the squire and the peasant.

1901

Spain

The Spaniards, to whom democratic institutions carry with them the hope of some great new advance and amelioration, regarded [King] Alfonso as an obstacle to their progress. The British and French democracies ... regarded the king as a sportsman; the Spaniards knew him as a ruler.

1931

Sudan

At once slovenly and uxorious, [the Sudanese soldier] detested his drills and loved his wives with equal earnestness.

1899[1]

From the growing workshops at Wady Halfa the continued clatter and clang of hammers and the black smoke of manufacture rose to the African sky. The malodorous incense of civilisation was offered to the startled gods of Egypt.

1899[2] *WSC had doubts about industry in unspoilt places.*

'Mad fanaticism' is the depreciating comment of [the Dervish's] conquerors ... Why should we regard as madness in the savage what would be sublime in civilised man?
1899[3]

United States of America
What an extraordinary people the Americans are! Their hospitality is a revelation to me and they make you feel at home and at ease in a way that I have never before experienced.
1895[1]

I paid my fare across Brooklyn Bridge with a paper dollar, I should think the most disreputable 'coin' the world has ever seen.
1895[2]

... the essence of American journalism is vulgarity divested of truth.
1895[3]

England and America are divided by a great ocean of salt water, but united by an eternal bathtub of soap and water.
1900[4]

I do not want to have too close an itinerary [for my American journey.] One must have time to feel a country and nibble some of the grass.
1929[5]

Few lines are drawn [in Britain] that are not smudged. Across the ocean it is all crisp and sharp.
1931[6]

I must confess that on one occasion I was taken to a 'speakeasy'. I went, of course, in my capacity as a Social Investigator.
1932[7]

Prohibition became effective in 1920. Many people must have had very large and well-stocked cellars in those distant days, and these supplies have lasted extremely well. Indeed one might almost believe that, like the widow's cruse, they miraculously replenish themselves.

1933[8] *The widow's cruse (pot), which never ran out of oil, appears in I Kings XVII 12–16.*

Pray bear this to your father from me. Tell him this must be the currency of the future.

1933[9] *WSC drew an intertwined pound and dollar sign which he referred to as the 'Sterling Dollar'. James Roosevelt asked, what if his father wished to call it the 'Dollar Sterling'? WSC replied with a smile, 'It is all the same.'*

The British Empire and the United States will have to be somewhat mixed up together in some of their affairs for mutual and general advantage … Like the Mississippi, it just keeps rolling along.

1940[10] *WSC sang 'Ol' Man River' all the way back to Downing Street in the car after his BBC broadcast of this speech.*

The Lend and Lease Bill must be regarded without question as the most unsordid act in the whole of recorded history.
1941[11]

Oh! That is the way we talked to her while we were wooing her; now that she is in the harem, we talk to her quite differently!

1941[12] *A colleague had urged a polite, careful dialogue with the United States following Pearl Harbor.*

I cannot help reflecting that if my father had been American and my mother British instead of the other way round, I might have got here [U.S. Congress] on my own. In that case, this would not have been the first time you would have heard my voice. In that case, I should not have needed any invitation, but if I had, it is hardly likely it would have been unanimous.
1941[13]

WSC: I saw [Niagara Falls] before you were born. I came here first in 1900.

    Reporter: Do they look the same?

    WSC: Well, the principle seems the same. The water still keeps falling over.

1943[14]

Great Britain and the United States all one? Yes, I am all for that, and you mean me to run for President?

1943[15]

The Americans can always be trusted to do the right thing, once all other possibilities have been exhausted.

circa 1944 *Churchill would never have said this publicly, and it is not in any memoirs of his colleagues. I include it as among the 'possibles,' since he certainly had those sentiments from time to time in World War II.*

Toilet paper too thin, newspapers too fat!

1944[16]

Why not put the eagle's neck on a swivel so that it could turn to the right or left as the occasion presented itself?

1946[17] *President Truman had revised the President's Seal so the eagle faced the olive branch of peace instead of the arrows of war.*

There is one country where a man knows he has an unbounded future: the USA, even though I deplore some of your habits ... You stop drinking with your meals.[18]

I could never run for President of the United States. All that handshaking of people I didn't give a damn about would kill me. Ten minutes here. Ten minutes there ... Not for me.

circa 1949[19]

I am told that a Boston lunch party is greatly to be preferred to a Boston Tea Party.

1949[20]

Their national psychology is such that the bigger the Idea the more wholeheartedly and obstinately do they throw themselves into making it a success. It is an admirable characteristic, providing the Idea is good.

1952[21]

[Discussing his American ancestors:] I was on both sides in the war between us and we.

1952[22]

We must be very careful nowadays – I perhaps all the more, because of my American forebears – in what we say about the American constitution. I will therefore content myself with the observation that no constitution was written in better English.

1953[23] *The British Constitution is, of course, unwritten…!*

I want no criticism of America at my table. The Americans criticise themselves more than enough.

1950s[24]

I am not going to choose between Republicans and Democrats. I want the lot!

1954[25]

Yugoslavia

Do you intend to make your home in Yugoslavia after the war? [Fitzroy Maclean: 'No.'] Neither do I. That being so, don't you think we had better leave it to the Yugoslavs to work out their own form of government? What concerns us most now is who is doing the most damage to the Germans.

1943 *WSC to Fitzroy Maclean (see People), who had reminded him that Tito's partisans, whom Churchill was supporting, were communist-led.*

9. War

Churchill observed or fought in wars from the Cuban rebellion of 1895 to World War II. Restricting this collection to 'witty' sayings may tend to minimise his profound revulsion for war and his lifelong efforts to forestall it; yet, at the same time, even his witticisms convey profound points.

He sadly concluded that 'the story of the human race is war', and, at least before the advent of apocalyptic nuclear weapons, regarded it as a recurring phenomenon. His precepts were simple: take the initiative, accept risk, prefer action to inaction, never give in until victory is won. Yet victory must be followed by magnanimity. He respected gallant foes, from the Boers in South Africa to Rommel in North Africa, but despised the treacherous, among whom Hitler was paramount.

In an age when declaring war is no longer fashionable, but wars exist all over the world, Churchill has much to tell us about the direction of military departments, the element of chance, the inevitability of mistakes, and the certainty of disappointments before victory is won.

Admirals

It is dangerous to meddle with Admirals when they say they can't do things. They have always got the weather or fuel or something to argue about.

1941

Air Power

The flying peril is not a peril from which one can fly. It is necessary to face it where we stand. We cannot possibly retreat. We cannot move London.

1934[1]

Hitler made a contract with the demon of the air, but the contract ran out before the job was done, and the demon has taken on an engagement with the rival firm.

1942[2]

Man has parted company with his trusty friend the horse and has sailed into the azure with the eagles, eagles being represented by the infernal [loud laughter] – er, I mean *internal* – combustion engine, ah, *engine* ... Even elderly Parliamentarians like myself are forced to acquire a high degree of mobility.

1943[3]

Allies
In working with Allies it sometimes happens that they develop opinions of their own.

1942

Army
The army was not an inanimate substance, it was a living thing. Regiments were not like houses ... They were more like plants: they grew slowly if they were to grow strong; they were easily affected by conditions of temperature and soil; and if they were blighted or transplanted they were apt to wither, and then they could only be revived by copious floods of public money.

1904

Artillery
Now I must say something about the artillery. I've had very little help from our Chairman [Alan Brooke] because he was mostly on the bow and arrow; after that we got to the musketoon and the tripod ...

1953

Bedding down

I was soon awakened by firing ... I fortified myself by dwelling on the fact that the Spanish officer whose hammock was slung between me and the enemy's fire was a man of substantial physique ... I have never been prejudiced against fat men ... Gradually I dropped asleep.

1930[1]

Colonel Byng and I shared a blanket. When he turned over I was in the cold. When I turned over I pulled the blanket off him and he objected. He was the Colonel. It was not a good arrangement. I was glad when morning came.

1930[2] *The Colonel was later Lord Byng of Vimy, who commended the Canadian Army Corps on the Western Front (1916–7) and was Governor General of Canada (1921–6).*

Boer War

Keep cool men! This will be interesting for my paper!

1899[1]

Sir, – I have the honour to inform you that as I do not consider that your Government have any right to detain me as a military prisoner, I have decided to escape from your custody ... Regretting that I am unable to bid you a more ceremonious or a personal farewell, I have the honour, to be, Sir, Your most obedient servant, Winston Churchill.

1899[2] *WSC to M. de Souza, Secretary of War, South African Republic, before he escaped from Boer clutches in Pretoria.*

My sole companion was a gigantic vulture, who manifested an extravagant interest in my condition, and made hideous and ominous gurglings from time to time.

1899[3]

Cavalry

It is a shame that War should have flung all this aside in its greedy, base, opportunist march, and should turn instead to chemists in spectacles, and chauffeurs pulling levers of airplanes or machine guns.

1930

Death by bombing

The guests must come prepared to meet their Maker, bearing in mind the heavy odds against such a meeting.

1944 WSC had invited the King and Cabinet to dinner on the eve of the new session of Parliament. He asked Lord Cherwell to work out the chances of being bombed. Cherwell gave the odds as 648,000 to one.

Democracy in wartime

The duty of a democracy in wartime is not to conceal but to confuse, 'not the silence of the oyster serene in its grotto, but the smudge and blur of the cuttlefish'.

1943

Deterrence

All attempts to bridge a twelve-foot stream by an eight-foot plank are doomed to failure, and the plank is lost. It is a concession, no doubt, to bring forward a nine-foot plank, but again that may be lost.

1938

Enemy, handling the

Lord Birkenhead mentioned to me a Latin quotation which seems to embody this idea extremely well. '*Parcere subjectis et debellare superbos*', which he translated finely, 'Spare the conquered and war down the proud'. I seem to have come very near achieving this thought by my own untutored reflections. The Romans have often forestalled many of my best ideas, and I must concede to them the patent rights in this maxim.

1930[1]

Let 'em have it. Remember this. Never maltreat the enemy by halves.

1940[2]

Generals

I have been told that in the British Army there are fewer bayonets and fewer sabres per general than in any other army in the world, except the Venezuelan army.

1903[1]

Those gilded and gorgeous functionaries with brass hats and ornamental duties who multiplied so luxuriously on the plains of Aldershot and Salisbury.

1905[2]

Infantry

When I was a soldier, infantry used to walk and cavalry used to ride. But now the infantry require motor-cars, and even the tanks have to have horse boxes to take them to battle.

1943

Military branches

You may take the most gallant sailor, the most intrepid airman, or the most audacious soldier, put them at a table together – what do you get? The sum of their fears.

1943[1]

'It would seem,' as I wrote, 'that the sum of all American fears is to be multiplied by the sum of all British fears, faithfully contributed by each Service.'

1951[2]

Navy, American

Who said a Wasp couldn't sting twice?

1942 *The aircraft carrier USS* Wasp *made two trips to Malta, laden with Spitfires for the island's defence.* Wasp *was sunk by Japanese torpedoes on 15 September 1942.*

Nuclear Deterrent

The argument is now put forward that we must never use the atomic bomb until, or unless, it has been used against us first. In other words, you must never fire until you have been shot dead.
1950

Officers

Many congratulations on becoming an officer and a gentleman. Don't let the double promotion go to your head.
1895[1] *WSC to Charles Maclean, who, like WSC, was commissioned in 1895.*

Laugh a little, and teach your men to laugh – great good humour under fire – war is a game that is played with a smile. If you can't smile, grin. If you can't grin, keep out of the way till you can.
1916[2]

Reflections on War

How easy to do nothing. How hard to achieve anything. War is action, energy & hazard. These sheep only want to browse among the daisies.
1916[1] *WSC to his wife, referring to the British wartime coalition government, which had excluded him.*

War, which used to be cruel and magnificent, has now become cruel and squalid.
1930[2]

We have had nothing else but wars since democracy took charge.
1947[3]

... little did we guess that what has been called The Century of the Common Man would witness as its outstanding feature more common men killing each other with greater facilities than any other five centuries put together in the history of the world. 1949[4]

Royal Naval College

WCS: Hello, Dickie, enjoying your supper? Any complaints?

Dickie, later Lord Mountbatten: 'Well, yes sir. We get only two sardines for supper on Sunday, we would sooner have three.' Admiral, make a note. These young gentlemen want *three* sardines for supper on Sunday, not two!

1913[1]

Don't you know that you are laying impious hands on the Ark of the Covenant? Don't you know that this naval system has existed since Nelson?

1941[2] *Robert Menzies had expressed disappointment with the management of the Royal Naval College.*

Sea battle

Indeed, the more we force ourselves to picture the hideous course of a modern naval engagement, the more one is inclined to believe that it will resemble the contest between Mamilius and Herminius at the battle of Lake Regillus, or the still more homely conflict of the Kilkenny cats.

1912[1] *Lake Regillus was a supposed Roman victory, led by Mamilius over Herminius and the Etruscans, possibly between 509 and 493 BC. The Kilkenny cats were fabled to have fought until only their tails remained.*

If you want to make a true picture in your mind of a battle between great modern ironclad ships you must not think of it as if it were two men in armour striking at each other with heavy swords. It is more like a battle between two egg-shells striking each other with hammers.

1914[2]

Submarine hunting

One knows that if you want a big bag of pheasants you beat them out of the cover in twos and threes, whereas if it is intended to shoot the cover over again the whole lot should be driven out as quickly as possible in the largest numbers. If rabbits run across a ride past a limited number of guns, their best chance is to run unexpectedly and all at once.

1917[1]

There are two people who sink U-boats in this war, Talbot. You sink them in the Atlantic and I sink them in the House of Commons. The trouble is that you are sinking them at exactly half the rate I am.

circa 1941[2]

Tanks

As might be expected, [the A.22 tank] had many defects and teething troubles, and when these became apparent the tank was appropriately rechristened the 'Churchill'. These defects have now been largely overcome.

1942[1]

What has happened to the amphibious tank? Surely a float or galosh can be made to take a tank of the larger size across the Channel under good conditions once a beach landing has been secured.

1943[2]

Under fire

Be calm! Nobody is ever wounded twice in the same day.

1899[1] *WSC's advice to the engineer during the ambush of his armoured train.*

… the bullet is brutally indiscriminating, and before it the brain of a hero or the quarters of a horse stand exactly the same chance to the vertical square inch.

1900[2]

World War I

At the beginning of this War megalomania was the only form of sanity.
1915[1]

War is declared, gentlemen, on the lice.
1916[2] *Churchill's first words to the Sixth Royal Scots Fusiliers, when he took command of the battalion in France. One of his officers, Andrew Dewar Gibb, added: 'With these words was inaugurated such a discourse on pulex Europaeus, its origin, growth and nature, its habitat and its importance as a factor in wars ancient and modern, as left one agape with wonder at the force of its author.'*

God for a month of power & a good shorthand writer.
1916[3]

… every offensive lost its force as it proceeded. It was like throwing a bucket of water over the floor. It first rushed forward, then soaked forward, and finally stopped altogether until another bucket could be brought.
1918[4]

The vials of wrath were full: but so were the reservoirs of power.
1923[5]

I remember at the Ministry of Munitions being told that we were running short of … bauxite and steel, and so forth; but we went on, and, in the end, the only thing we ran short of was Huns.
1941[6]

World War II prelude

The Romans had a maxim: 'Shorten your weapons and lengthen your frontiers.' But our maxim seems to be: 'Diminish your weapons and increase your obligations.' Aye, and 'diminish the weapons of your friends'.
1934[1]

With our enormous Metropolis here, the greatest target in the world, a kind of tremendous, fat, valuable cow tied up to attract the beast of prey, we are in a position in which we have never been before, and in which no other country in the world is at the present time.

1934[2]

[French Foreign Minister Pierre] Laval said: 'Can't you do something to encourage religion and the Catholics in Russia? It would help me so much with the Pope.' 'Oho!' said Stalin. 'The Pope! How many divisions has he got?' Laval's answer was not reported to me; but he might certainly have mentioned a number of legions not always visible on parade.

1935[3]

The world seems to be divided between the confident nations who behave harshly, and the nations who have lost confidence in themselves and behave fatuously.

1936[4]

A friend of mine the other day saw a number of persons engaged in peculiar evolutions, genuflections and gestures ... He wondered whether it was some novel form of gymnastics, or a new religion ... or whether they were a party of lunatics out for an airing ... they were a Searchlight Company of London Territorials, who were doing their exercises as well as they could without having the searchlights.

1936[5]

Well, I suppose they asked me to show him [Ribbentrop] that, if they couldn't bite themselves, they kept a dog who could bark and might bite.

1938[6] *The Cabinet had asked Churchill to join them for lunch to bid farewell to Hitler's Ambassador Joachim von Ribbentrop, while Austria was being absorbed by Germany.*

... this great country [is] nosing from door to door like a cow that has lost its calf, mooing dolefully now in Berlin and now in Rome – when all the time the tiger and the alligator wait for its undoing.

1938[7]

... we seem to be very near the bleak choice between War and Shame. My feeling is that we shall choose Shame, and then have War thrown in a little later on even more adverse terms than at present.

1938[8] *WSC to Lord Moyne (and not, as frequently stated, to Chamberlain in Parliament).*

I think I hear something ... the tramp of two million German soldiers and more than a million Italians – going on manoeuvres – yes, only on manoeuvres ... just like last year. After all, the Dictators must train their soldiers. They could scarcely do less in common prudence, when the Danes, the Dutch, the Swiss, the Albanians – and of course the Jews – may leap out upon them at any moment and rob them of their living-space ...

1939[9]

World War II

... a strange, prolonged, wailing noise, afterwards to become familiar, broke upon the ear ... We made our way to the shelter assigned to us, armed with a bottle of brandy and other appropriate medical comforts.

1939[1]

Such is the U-boat war – hard, widespread and bitter, a war of groping and drowning, a war of ambuscade and stratagem, a war of science and seamanship.

1939[2]

... the Royal Navy has immediately attacked the U-boats, and is hunting them night and day – I will not say without mercy, because God forbid we should ever part company with that, but at any rate with zeal and not altogether without relish.
1939[3]

... thoughtless dilettanti or purblind wordlings who sometimes ask us: 'What is it that Britain and France are fighting for?' To this I answer: 'If we left off fighting you would soon find out.'
1940[4]

I thought of Wellington's mood in the afternoon of the Battle of Waterloo: 'Would God that night or Blucher would come.' This time we did not want Blucher.
1940[5]

There is really no good sense in having these prolonged banshee howlings from sirens two or three times a day over wide areas, simply because hostile aircraft are flying to or from some target which no one can possibly know or even guess ... most people now see how very wise Ulysses was when he stopped the ears of his sailors from all siren songs and had himself tied up firmly to the mast of duty.
1940[6]

It is curious that in this war I have had no success but have received nothing but praise, whereas in the last war I did several things which I thought were good and got nothing but abuse for them.
1940[7] *Reconstructed in the first person from John Colville's diary for 31 August 1940. Among the abuse for things he thought good in World War I were his commanding the defence of Antwerp and supporting the Dardanelles campaign in 1915.*

One [bomb] squad [comprised] the Earl of Suffolk, his lady private secretary, and his rather aged chauffeur. They called themselves 'the Holy Trinity' ... Thirty-four unexploded bombs did they tackle with urbane and smiling efficiency. But the thirty-fifth claimed its forfeit. Up went the Earl of Suffolk in his Holy Trinity. But we may be sure that ... 'all the trumpets sounded for them on the other side'.

1940[8]

[Graziani] was indignant that he should have been forced into so hazardous an advance upon Egypt by Rommel's undue influence on Mussolini. He complained that he had been forced into a struggle between 'a flea and an elephant'. Apparently the flea had devoured a large portion of the elephant.

1940[9] *The advance of Gen. Rodolfo Graziani towards Cairo was halted by Gen. Richard O'Connor's Western Desert Force, with the loss of five Italian divisions.*

I am, of course, aware that a mechanised army makes an enormous additional drain ... I have thought nevertheless for some time that the Army and Air Force – the Navy not so much – have a great need to comb their tails in order to magnify their teeth.

1941[10]

I must say a word about the function of the Minister charged with the study of post-war problems and reconstruction. It is not his task to make a new world, comprising a new Heaven, a new earth, and no doubt a new hell (as I am sure that would be necessary in any balanced system).

1941[11]

I think we should have to retain a certain amount of power in the selection of the music. Very spirited renderings of 'Deutschland Uber Alles' would hardly be permissible.

1941[12]

This war would never have come unless, under American and modernising pressure, we had driven the Hapsburgs out of Austria and Hungary and the Hohenzollerns out of Germany. By making these vacuums we gave the opening for the Hitlerite monster to crawl out of its sewer on to the vacant thrones. No doubt these views are very unfashionable.

1941[13]

They must float up and down with the tide ... Let me have the best solution worked out. Don't argue the matter. The difficulties will argue for themselves.

1941[14] *Prime Minister to Chief of Combined Operations on what became the floating Mulberry Harbours used in the Normandy invasion – but Churchill had proposed the same idea for an invasion of Germany in 1917.*

I have only one single purpose – the destruction of Hitler – and my life is much simplified thereby. If Hitler invaded Hell I would at least make a favourable reference to the Devil in the House of Commons.

1941[15] *Hitler had invaded Russia. Reconstructed in the first person from Sir John Colville's diaries.*

We will have no truce or parley with you, or the grisly gang who work your wicked will. You do your worst – and we will do our best. Perhaps it may be our turn soon; perhaps it may be our turn now.

1941[16]

A handful of Members can fill a couple of days' debate with disparaging charges against our war effort, and every ardent or disaffected section of the Press can take it up, and the whole can cry a dismal cacophonous chorus of stinking fish all round the world.

1941[17]

It is twenty-seven years ago today that Huns began their last war. We must make a good job of it this time. Twice ought to be enough.

1941[18] *WSC to Roosevelt, leaving for their Atlantic meeting at Placentia Bay, Newfoundland.*

It is a month ago that I remarked upon the long silence of Herr Hitler, a remark which apparently provoked him to make a speech in which he told the German people that Moscow would fall in a few days. That shows, as everyone I am sure will agree, how much wiser he would have been to go on keeping his mouth shut.

1941[19]

I am the most miserable Englishman in America – since Burgoyne.

1942[20] *Churchill had been informed of the surrender of Tobruk. General John Burgoyne (1722–1792) surrendered to the Americans at Saratoga on 17 October 1777.*

The hen has been part and parcel of the country cottager's life since history began. Townsfolk can eke out their rations by a bought meal.

1942[21]

I visited the Alamein positions ... Thence we proceeded along the front to his headquarters behind the Ruweisat Ridge, where we were given breakfast in a wire-netted cube, full of flies and important military personages.

1942[22]

1. Your prime and main duty will be to take or destroy at the earliest opportunity the German-Italian Army commanded by Field Marshal Rommel, together with all its supplies and establishments in Egypt and Libya. 2. You will discharge or cause to be discharged such other duties as pertain to your Command

without prejudice to the task described in paragraph 1, which must be considered paramount in His Majesty's interests.

1942[23] *Prime Minister to General Alexander, Commander-in-Chief, Middle East. In February 1943, Field Marshal Alexander replied. See below.*

General Alexander to Prime Minister, February 1943: 'Sir: The Orders you gave me on August [10], 1942, have been fulfilled. His Majesty's enemies, together with their impedimenta, have been completely eliminated from Egypt, Cyrenaica, Libya, and Tripolitania. I now await your further instructions.'

WSC: Well, obviously, we shall have to think of something else.

1943[24]

...our chickens are not yet hatched, though one can hear them pecking at their shells.

1943[25]

I drink to the Proletarian masses.

Stalin: 'I drink to the Conservative Party.'

1943[26] *Toasts at a dinner for FDR and Stalin hosted by Churchill on his birthday.*

There I sat with the great Russian bear on one side of me, with paws outstretched, and on the other side the great American buffalo and between the two sat the poor little English donkey who was the only one, the only one of the three, who knew the right way home.

1944[27]

... I had hoped that we were hurling a wild cat on to the shore [at Anzio], but all we got was a stranded whale.

1944[28]

A small lion was walking between a huge Russian bear and a great American elephant, but perhaps it will prove to be the lion who knew the way.

1945[29] *Describing the Yalta Conference to John Colville, Czech President Beneš and Foreign Secretary Masaryk.*

Hitler, personally.

1945[30] *WSC wrote this greeting on a 240 mm shell during his visit to the Rhine front.*

I deem it highly important that we should shake hands with the Russians as far to the east as possible.

1945[31]

… I therefore beg, Sir, with your permission to move 'That this House do now attend at the church of St Margaret, Westminster, to give humble and reverent thanks to Almighty God for our deliverance from the threat of German domination.' This is the identical motion which was moved in former times.

1945[32]

It shows that if you get into a war, it is supremely important to win it. You and I would be in a pretty pickle if we had lost.

1946[33] *WSC to General Ismay, referring to the results of the Nuremberg trials.*

They [British code-breakers] were the geese who laid the golden eggs and never cackled.

1940s[34]

A gentleman, Mr Thomson, kindly presented me with a lion … 'Rota' … was a male lion of fine quality and in eight years became the father of many children. The assistant secretary who had been with me in the airplane came with some papers. He was a charming man, highly competent, but physically on the small side. Indulging in chaff, I now showed him a magnificent photograph of Rota with his mouth open, saying, 'If there are any shortcomings in your work I shall send you to him. Meat is very short now.' He took a serious view of this remark. He reported to the office that I was in a delirium.

1951[35]

10. Politics and Government

Herein Churchill applies his wit to the conduct of governments from Bolshevik to Nazi, dictatorships to democracies. We know how highly he held British Parliamentary democracy. As a young man he read Parliamentary debates for the past fifty years, gaining familiarity with the language, demeanour and courtesies of the House of Commons: a member of the Privy Council was 'Rt. Hon.', one of his own party 'Hon. Friend', an MP who had served in the forces was 'Hon. and Gallant', a legal scholar was 'Hon. and Learned'. Rarely if ever did he forget the protocol of his 'natural home'.

Churchill did not say what people wanted to hear, but what he thought they *should* hear. His approach to both domestic and international politics was consistent: to fight with might and main while the battle is engaged, but to be magnanimous in victory.

Though he had barbed words for political opponents, he believed in courtesy off the floor – and coalitions in times of extreme danger (but not in the peacetime 1930s, when he believed they stultified debate and destroyed sound policy). He favoured light taxation, a medium between the extremes of Left and Right, relying upon the British democracy to ensure equality and a decent life for all. He was a patrician, but not a snob; he enjoyed luxuries, but believed in taxing them; though he found fault with democracy, he always respected the 'little man'. Justice and equality were prominent among his principles.

Bank of England

Mon Général, devant la vieille dame de Threadneedle Street je suis impotent.

1940 *Desmond Morton to John Colville, recording WSC's response when General Sikorski asked for supplies of foreign exchange for Polish forces.*

The 'Old Lady of Threadneedle Street' is a long-time sobriquet for the Bank of England.

Bolshevism and Communism

If I had been properly supported in 1919, I think we might have strangled Bolshevism in its cradle, but everybody turned up their hands and said, 'How shocking!'
1954[1]

The Communist theme aims at universal standardisation ... The Beehive? No, for there must be no queen and no honey, or at least no honey for others.
1931[2]

Trying to maintain good relations with a Communist is like wooing a crocodile. You do not know whether to tickle it under the chin or to beat it over the head. When it opens its mouth you cannot tell whether it is trying to smile or preparing to eat you up.
1944[3]

Budget Excesses

Squandermania ... is the policy which used to be stigmatised by the late Mr Thomas Gibson Bowles as the policy of buying a biscuit early in the morning and walking about all day looking for a dog to give it to.
1929

Cartoons

Just as eels are supposed to get used to skinning, so politicians get used to being caricatured ... If we must confess it, they are quite offended and downcast when the cartoons stop ... They fear old age and obsolescence are creeping upon them. They murmur: 'We are not mauled and maltreated as we used to be. The great days are ended.'
1931

Communism vs Fascism

[They remind me] of the North Pole and the South Pole. They are at opposite ends of the earth, but if you woke up at either Pole tomorrow morning you could not tell which one it was.
1937[1]

I will not pretend that, if I had to choose between Communism and Nazism, I would choose Communism. I hope not to be called upon to survive in the world under a government of either of those dispensations.
1937[2]

Debate

... some people's idea of it [debate] is that they are free to say what they like, but if anyone says anything back, that is an outrage.
1943[1]

Disagreement is much more easy to express, and often much more exciting to the reader, than agreement.
1954[2]

Democracy

Democracy is no harlot to be picked up in the street by a man with a tommy gun.
1944

Diplomacy

[I insist] that I be host at dinner tomorrow evening. I think I have one or two claims to precedence. To begin with, I come first in seniority and alphabetically. In the second place, I represent the longest established of the three governments. And, in the third place, tomorrow happens to be my birthday.
1943 *WSC to W. Averell Harriman, US Ambassador to Russia, 1943–6. WSC was perhaps too diplomatic to add that Britain had been fighting longer, too.*

Election, 1945

This may well be a landslide and [the Labour Party] have a perfect right to kick us out. That is democracy. That is what we have been fighting for. Hand me my towel.

1945[1] *WSC to Captain Richard Pim, his wartime map-keeper, as the first dozen election results came in, strongly against the Conservative Party.*

A friend of mine, an officer, was in Zagreb when the results of the late General Election came in. An old lady said to him, 'Poor Mr Churchill! I suppose now he will be shot.' My friend was able to reassure her. He said the sentence might be mitigated to one of the various forms of hard labour which are always open to His Majesty's subjects.

1945[2] *The officer was WSC's literary assistant Bill Deakin, then Col. Deakin.*

Elections

At the bottom of all the tributes paid to democracy is the little man, walking into the little booth, with a little pencil, making a little cross on a little bit of paper – no amount of rhetoric or voluminous discussion can possibly diminish the overwhelming importance of that point.

1944

Expenditure

Expenditure always is popular; the only unpopular part about it is the raising of the money to pay the expenditure.

1901

Foreign Policy: Mideast and Africa

In the Middle East you have arid countries. In East Africa you have dripping countries. There is the greatest difficulty to get anything to grow in the one place, and the greatest difficulty to prevent things smothering and choking you by their hurried growth in the other. In the African Colonies you have a docile, tractable population, who only require to be well and wisely treated to develop great economic capacity and utility; whereas the regions of the Middle East are unduly stocked with peppery, pugnacious, proud politicians and theologians, who happen to be at the same time extremely well armed and extremely hard up.

1921

General Strike, 1926

… make your minds perfectly clear that if ever you let loose upon us again a General Strike, we will loose upon you [catcalls and uproar] – another *British Gazette*!

1926[1] *As WSC reached his punch line, referring to the government paper he had produced when the strike closed the regular newspapers, the jeers dissolved into laughter.*

I decline utterly to be impartial as between the fire brigade and the fire.

1926[2]

Gold Standard

… when I am talking to bankers and economists, after a while they begin to talk Persian, and then they sink me instead.

1924[1]

The Gold Standard is no more responsible for the condition of affairs in the coal industry than is the Gulf Stream.

1925[2]

Government, World War II

Except for you and me, this is the worst Government England ever had!

1943 *WSC to Anthony Eden.*

House of Commons
The [party] system is much favoured by the oblong form of Chamber. It is easy for an individual to move through those insensible gradations from Left to Right, but the act of crossing the floor is one which requires serious consideration. I am well informed on this matter, for I have accomplished that difficult process not only once but twice. Logic is a poor guide compared with custom. Logic, which has created in so many countries semi-circular assemblies with buildings that give to every Member, not only a seat to sit in, but often a desk to write at, with a lid to bang, has proved fatal to Parliamentary Government as we know it here in its home and in the land of its birth.
1943

House of Lords
[The Conservatives] will have to defend this Second Chamber as it is – one-sided, hereditary, unpurged, unrepresentative, irresponsible, absentee.
1907[1]

[Peers] have got rather roughly mauled in [the Lords debate]. Do not let us be too hard on them. It is poor sport almost like teasing goldfish … These ornamental creatures blunder on every hook they see, and there is no sport whatever in trying to catch them. It would be barbarous to leave them gasping on the bank of public ridicule upon which they have landed themselves. Let us put them back gently, tenderly into their fountains and if a few bright gold scales have been rubbed off in what the Prime Minister calls the variegated handling they have received, they will soon get over it.
1909[2]

Housing and parks

… I'd like the houses of the poor people south of the River [Thames] rebuilt and a great park, like Battersea Park, prepared for the kiddies, with lots of ponds full of sticklebacks and many fountains.

1944

Interruptions

The Hon. Gentleman [Mr Logan] … has arrogated to himself a function which did not belong to him, namely, to make my speech instead of letting me make it.

1931

Judges

What would be thought of a Lord Chief Justice if he won the Derby? [Laughter.] Yet I could cite a solid precedent where such an act had been perpetrated by a Prime Minister who, on the whole, had got away with it all right. [Laughter.]

1954 *Although the laughter was in the knowledge that he himself kept a racing stable, WSC was referring to Lord Rosebery (Prime Minister 1894–5), whose horses, Ladas and Sir Visto, won the Derby in 1894 and 1895.*

Meetings, conduct of

An empty bladder is the indispensable prelude to a fruitful discussion.

1950 *After several elderly gentlemen had excused themselves for toilet, WSC adjourned the meeting for five minutes with this declaration. The then Michael Fraser was a young note-taker at the meeting.*

Moderates

They are a class of Rt. Hon. Gentlemen – all good men, all honest men – who are ready to make great sacrifices for their opinions, but they have no opinions. They are ready to die for the truth, if they only knew what the truth was.

1903

Monarchy

The Socialists are quite in favour of the Monarchy, and make generous provisions for it ... They even go to the parties at Buckingham Palace. Those who have very extreme principles wear sweaters.

1947

Opposition

Call them not 'the Party opposite', but 'the Party in that corner!'

1906[1]

In England we even pay the Leader of the Opposition a salary of £2000 a year to make sure that the Government is kept up to the mark. I have no doubt that Mr Attlee ... will devote himself to his constitutional task with the zeal which, under totalitarian systems, might well lead him to Siberia or worse.

1952[2]

Parliament

It is quite true that nothing can bind a Parliament. Every Parliament is entirely free to behave like a gentleman or like a cad; every Parliament is entirely free to behave honestly or like a crook. Such are the sovereign rights of this august assembly.

1948

Party splitting

Splitting an infinitive isn't so bad – not nearly so bad – hmph, as splitting a party; that is always regarded as the greatest sin.

1946

Planning

Ah! Yes! I know: town planning – densities, broad vistas, open spaces. Give me the romance of the 18th-century alley, with its dark corners, where footpads lurk.

1942

Political cause and effect

Militarism degenerates into brutality. Loyalty promotes tyranny and sycophancy. Humanitarianism becomes maudlin and ridiculous. Patriotism shades into cant. Imperialism sinks to jingoism.

1898

Political parties

The alternation of Parties in power, like the rotation of crops, has beneficial results.

1907

Politicians

[A politician] is asked to stand, he wants to sit and he is expected to lie.

1902[1]

For my own part I have always felt that a politician is to be judged by the animosities which he excites among his opponents. I have always set myself not merely to relish but to deserve thoroughly their censure.

1906[2]

Polls

I see [it] said that leaders should keep their ears to the ground. All I can say is that the British nation will find it very hard to look up to the leaders who are detected in that somewhat ungainly posture.

1941

Poverty

Fancy living in one of those streets – never seeing anything beautiful – never eating anything savoury – never saying anything clever!

1908 *WSC to his private secretary Eddie Marsh, as they walked through a poor section of Manchester, where he was standing for Parliament.*

Prime Minister

The dignity of a Prime Minister, like a lady's virtue, is not susceptible of partial diminution.

1905

Private enterprise

Among our Socialist opponents there is great confusion. Some of them regard private enterprise as a predatory tiger to be shot. Others look on it as a cow they can milk. [Here WSC made the motion of milking a cow with his hands.] Only a handful see it for what it really is – the strong and willing horse that pulls the whole cart along.

1959

Revolution

Those who talk of revolution ought to be prepared for the guillotine.

1912

Socialists

How many political flibbertigibbets are there not running up and down the land calling themselves the people of Great Britain, and the social democracy, and the masses of the nation!

1906[1]

They keep the British bulldog running round after his own tail till he is dizzy and then wonder that he cannot keep the wolf from the door.

1948[2]

Never before in the history of human government has such great havoc been wrought by such small men.

1949[3]

Summit conferences

… when I have the rare and fortunate chance to meet the President of the United States, we are not limited in our discussions by any sphere. We talk over the whole position in every aspect – the military, economic, diplomatic, financial. All is examined. And obviously that should be so. The fact that we have worked so long together, and the fact that we have got to know each other so well under the hard stresses of war, make the solution of problems so much simpler, so swift. What an ineffectual method of conveying human thought correspondence is – even when it is telegraphed with all the rapidity and all the facilities of modern intercommunication! They are simply dead blank walls compared to personal contacts.

1944 *Churchill who first spoke of a 'meeting at the summit'. Here he provides a splendid rationale.*

Taxation

It is a curious thing in our system of taxation how much easier it is to revive an old tax than to impose a new one.

1902[1]

Perhaps the House may remember that only seven or eight years ago I got into some trouble myself about the Kerosene Tax. It was a very good tax. I was quite right about it. My Rt. Hon. Friend [Neville Chamberlain] slipped it through a year or two later without the slightest trouble and it never ruined the homes of the people at all … I acted with great promptitude. In the nick of time, just as Mr Snowden [Chancellor of the Exchequer in the 1929 Labour government] was rising with overwhelming fury, I got up and withdrew [the tax on kerosene]. Was I humiliated? Was I accused of running away? No! Everyone said, 'How clever! How quick! How right!' Pardon me referring to it. It was one of my best days.

1937[2] *Chamberlain had just become Prime Minister; in his last budget as Chancellor he had proposed a tax which was severely criticised. Churchill's adroit speech helped Chamberlain withdraw the tax proposal.*

Vote of Confidence

The Government ask for a Vote of Confidence, but I hope they
will not make the mistake of thinking that it is a testimonial, or
a bouquet, or that it arises from long-pent-up spontaneous
feelings of enthusiasm which can no longer be held in check.
1936[1]

H – is a silly bastard. There are about half a dozen of them;
they make a noise out of all proportion to their importance.
The House knows this, but unfortunately people abroad take
them too seriously; they do a lot of harm. You know how they
voted? Four hundred and sixty-four to one.
1942[2]

Warmongering

I resented Mr Stalin calling [Mr Attlee] a warmonger. I thought
this was quite untrue. It was also unfair because the word
'warmonger' was, as you have no doubt heard, the one that
many of Mr Attlee's friends and followers were hoping to
fasten on me whenever the election comes … Stalin has
therefore been guilty, not only of an untruth, but of
infringement of copyright.
1951

War Office

The War Office is always preparing for the last war. I certainly
entered this war with a mentality born in the last war.
1942[1]

… I am going to do something that has never been done
before, and I hope the House will not be shocked at the breach
of precedent. I am going to make public a word of praise for
the War Office. In all the forty years I have served in this
House I have heard that Department steadily abused before,
during, and after our various wars. And if my memory serves

me aright I have frequently taken part in the well-merited criticism which was their lot.

1944[2]

Wisdom and Folly

… it would be a great reform in politics if wisdom could be made to spread as easily and as rapidly as folly.

1947

Women in politics

Even the women have votes … They are a strong prop to the Tories … It did not turn out as badly as I thought … Some of them have even been Ministers. There are not many of them. They have found their level … it has made politicians more mealy-mouthed than in your day. And public meetings are much less fun. You can't say the things you used to.

1947 *For the background of this piece, see Stories and Jokes, The Dream.*

11. Education,
Arts and Science

Churchill often regretted that he had not had a University education, and stood in confessed awe of those who did. It wasn't until he was approaching twenty-two that the 'desire for learning', as he wrote, 'began to press insistently upon me ... So I resolved to read history, philosophy, economics, and things like that; and I wrote to my mother asking for such books as I had heard of on these topics'.

Churchill had a lively interest in science, both military and civilian. What he said about energy independence, leaded paint and mosquito eradication, for example, is remarkably close to modern views. Thus he relied heavily on his friend Professor Lindemann, who could 'decipher the signals from the experts on the far horizons and explain to me in lucid, homely terms what the issues were'.

As a politician he was convinced of the importance of education, and pondered the 'information revolution' before that term had been coined. He read and devoured newspapers, but he considered them 'an education at once universal and superficial'.

Arts
[The Director of the National Gallery, Kenneth Clark, suggested that the paintings in the National Gallery should be sent from London to Canada for safekeeping.]

No – bury them in caves and cellars. None must go. We are going to beat them.
1940[1]

Art is to beauty what honour is to honesty, an unnatural allotropic form.
1899[2]

Cancer

You cannot cure cancer by a majority. What is wanted is a remedy.

1930

Classics

Men no longer study the classics. It was an advantage when there was one common discipline and every nation studied the doings of two states [Greece and Rome, one presumes]. Now they learn how to mend motorcars.

1945[1]

There is a good saying to the effect that when a new book appears one should read an old one. As an author I would not recommend too strict an adherence to this saying.

1948[2]

Disease

Man is a gregarious animal, and apparently the mischievous microbes he exhales fight and neutralise each other. They go out and devour each other, and Man walks off unharmed. If this is not scientifically correct, it ought to be.

1948

English

... by being so long in the lowest form [at Harrow] I gained an immense advantage over the cleverer boys ... I got into my bones the essential structure of the ordinary British Sentence – which is a noble thing ... Naturally I am biased in favour of boys learning English ... I would let the clever ones learn Latin as an honour, and Greek as a treat. But the only thing I would whip them for is not knowing English. I would whip them hard for that.

1930

Explosives

This is one of those rare and happy occasions when respectable people like you and me can enjoy pleasures normally reserved to the Irish Republican Army.

1940 *Churchill to Air Marshal Commodore John Slessor, while tinkering with a model bomb thought useful in mining the Rhine to stop German river traffic.*

Guided missiles

Do you understand, my dear? This Contraption seeks out the enemy. Smells him out. And devoid of human aid encompasses his destruction.

1952 *WSC to his wife.*

Latin

I was often uncertain whether the Ablative Absolute should end in 'e' or 'i' or 'o' or 'is' or 'ibus' ... Mr Welldon seemed to be physically pained by a mistake being made in any of these letters. I remember that later on Mr Asquith used to have just the same sort of look on his face when I sometimes adorned a Cabinet discussion by bringing out one of my few but faithful Latin quotations.

1930 *Bishop Welldon was WSC's Harrow Headmaster; H. H. Asquith was the first Prime Minister Churchill served in Cabinet.*

Metaphysics

I am also at this point accustomed to reaffirm with emphasis my conviction that the sun is real, and also that it is hot – in fact as hot as Hell, and that if the metaphysicians doubt it they should go there and see.

1930

Public Schools

I am all for the Public Schools but I do not want to go there again.
1930[1]

Hitler, in one of his recent discourses, declared that the fight was between those who have been through the Adolf Hitler Schools and those who have been at Eton. Hitler has forgotten Harrow.

1940[2]

RMS *Queen Mary*

Never in the whole history of Atlantic travel has so lavish provision been made for those who travel 'tourist'.

1936

Socrates

Who was Socrates, anyhow? A very argumentative Greek who had a nagging wife and was finally compelled to commit suicide because he was a nuisance! Still, he was beyond doubt a considerable person.

1896

Technology

We want a lot of engineers in the modern world, but we do not want a world of engineers. We want some scientists, but we must keep them in their proper place.

1948

Television

The television has come to take its place in the world; as a rather old-fashioned person I have not been one of its principal champions ...

1952[1]

Even though we have to sink to this level, we always have to keep pace with modern improvements.

1955[2] *Stated by Churchill when making a television screen test.*

12. Personal

Although Churchill liked to declaim against exercise, he was quite active until very late in his life, playing polo until his fifties and riding to hounds in his seventies. His perambulations around Chartwell were as good an aerobic exercise as any doctor would prescribe for a mature man.

Although he spoke modestly of what he called 'my daubs', his friend Sir John Lavery, an official artist in the First World War, said: 'Had he chosen painting instead of statesmanship, I believe he would have been a great master with the brush.'

Churchill was not given to religious observance, but he was not irreligious (see last entry under 'Religion' herein). He was introduced to religious diversity early, being brought up as 'High Church', but with a Nanny 'who enjoyed a very Low Church form of piety'. When in rebellious mood he would tell Nanny Everest 'the worst thing that he could think of … that he would go out and 'worship idols'.

Advice
What you say is very grandfatherly. You're always giving me grandfatherly advice. You're not my grandfather, you know.
1945 *WSC to his son Randolph.*

Afterlife (see also 'Death')
Everyone will have equal rights in Heaven. That will be the real Welfare State. And then there will be the cherubs. How strange it will be to have them around.
circa 1946[1]

Mr President, I hope you have your answer ready for that hour when you and I stand before St Peter and he says, 'I understand you two are responsible for putting off those atomic bombs.'

Robert Lovett: 'Are you sure, Prime Minister, that you are going to be in the same place as the President for that interrogation?'

WSC: Lovett, my vast respect for the Creator of this universe and countless others gives me assurance that He would not condemn a man without a hearing.

Lovett: True, but your hearing would not be likely to start in the Supreme Court, or necessarily in the same court as the President's. It could be in another court far away.

WSC: I don't doubt that, but, wherever it is, it will be in accordance with the principles of English Common Law.

1953[2]

He will take my skin with him, a kind of advance guard, into the next world.

1954[3] *On Richard Molyneux, a fellow soldier who had been wounded at Omdurman and had received a skin graft from Churchill at that time.*

Aging

WSC: Who is that?

Julian Amery: Morrison, he used to be your Home Secretary.

WSC: Are you sure? He looks very much aged!

1956

Alcohol

All I can say is that I have taken more out of alcohol than alcohol has taken out of me.[1]

Until this time [1899] I had never been able to drink whisky. I disliked the flavour intensely … I now found myself in heat which, though I stood it personally fairly well, was terrific, for five whole days and with absolutely nothing to drink, apart from tea, except either tepid water or tepid water with limejuice or tepid water with whisky. Faced with these alternatives I 'grasped the larger hope' … Wishing to fit myself for active service conditions I overcame the ordinary weaknesses of the flesh. By the end of those five days I had completely overcome my repugnance to the taste of whisky. Nor was this a momentary acquirement. On the contrary the ground I gained in those days I have firmly entrenched and held throughout my whole life.

1930[2]

WSC: Will you have a whisky and soda, Mr Prime Minister of Pakistan?

Nazimuddin, horrified: No, thank you! ... I'm a teetotaller, Mr Prime Minister.

WSC: A teetotaller! Christ! I mean God! I mean ALLAH!

1953[3] *Sir Khawaja Nazimuddin KCIE (1894–1964) was Pakistan's second Prime Minister (October 1951–April 1953).*

No, I am going to lunch at Buckingham Palace and it would not look well if I were to slither under the Royal table.

1942[4] *Declining sherry in the Commons smoking room.*

At the White House (Dry, alas!); with the Sultan. After dinner, recovery from the effects of the above.

1943[5] *WSC referred to Roosevelt's Villa Mirador as 'the White House'.*

I [have a] profound distaste on the one hand for skim milk and no deep rooted prejudice about wine ... [I have] reconciled the conflict in favour of the latter ...

1943[6]

There's a total abstainer died of gout. How right we all are!

1944[7] *On the death of William Temple, Archbishop of Canterbury.*

At this point I will take a little lubrication, if it is permissible. I think it is always a great pleasure to the Noble Lady, the Member for the Sutton Division of Plymouth [Lady Astor, a stern teetotaler] to see me drinking water.

1944[8]

I could not live without Champagne. In victory I deserve it. In defeat I need it.

1946[9] *WSC to Mme Odette Pol-Roger.*

I could have respected the ancient tradition of a dry Navy, but this tantalising business of the empty wine glass – and then this matter of too little and too late – I hope you don't follow such barbarous practices in your house, Franks!

1952[10] *To the British Ambassador Sir Oliver Franks during a visit to the White House.*

When I was younger I made it a rule never to take strong drink before lunch. It is now my rule never to do so before breakfast.

1952[11] *WSC to King George VI as they saw Princess Elizabeth and the Duke of Edinburgh off on what was intended to be a prolonged Commonwealth tour. The King died five days later.*

I neither want it nor need it but I should think it pretty hazardous to interfere with the ineradicable habit of a lifetime.

1953[12]

Ambition

WSC: ... if you are going to include all parties, you will have to have me in your new National Party.

Lloyd George: Oh no! To be a party you must have at least one follower. You have none.

1920

Ancestry

Adlai Stevenson: 'What message would you like me to bring from you to the English-Speaking Union?'

WSC: My mother was American, my ancestors were officers in Washington's army; so I am myself an English-Speaking Union.

1953

Animals

Dogs look up to you, cats look down on you. Give me a pig! He looks you in the eye and treats you as an equal.[1]

All the black swans are mating, not only the father and mother, but both brothers and both sisters have paired off. The Ptolemys always did this and Cleopatra was the result. At any rate I have not thought it my duty to interfere.

1935[2]

One of the heifers has committed an indiscretion before she came to us and is about to have a calf. I propose however to treat it as a daughter.

1935[3]

We cannot discriminate against the Russians over a bull ... But they'll have to pay a good price to get it. I'm not going to have that poor fellow sent to Russia for nothing.

circa 1946[4] *WSC had advertised a prize bull; the Russians professed interest.*

You carve [this goose], Clemmie. He was a friend of mine.

circa 1958[5]

Birth

It's an extraordinary business this way of bringing babies into the world. I don't know how God thought of it.

1954

Birthday Portrait

The portrait is a remarkable example of modern art. It certainly combines force and candour.

1954 This drew a laugh, but Churchill actually despised his portrait by Graham Sutherland, presented by both Houses of Parliament on his eightieth birthday. He so hated it that his wife had it burned.

Bishops

I would have you know that in this past year I have appointed no less than six bishops. If that is not spiritual inspiration, what is?

1942 WSC to Jan Smuts. who had charged WSC with failure to provide spiritual leadership. Lord Moran quotes WSC as saying, 'I have made more Bishops than anyone since St Augustine,' but Lord Tedder's version seems more likely.

Blood sample

You can use my finger, or my ear and, of course, I have an almost infinite expanse of arse.

1943

Cigars

How can I tell that the soothing influence of tobacco upon my nervous system may not have enabled me to comport myself with calm and with courtesy in some awkward personal encounter or negotiation, or carried me serenely through some critical hours of anxious waiting? How can I tell that my temper would have been as sweet or my companionship as agreeable if I had abjured from my youth the goddess Nicotine?

1931[1]

… of two cigars, pick the longest and the strongest.

undated[2]

Confidence

I'm like a bomber pilot. I go out night after night, and I know that one night I'll not return.

circa 1942[1] WSC to Malcolm MacDonald, discussing his ups and downs in the confidence of the country.

I have a very strong feeling that my work is done. I have no message. I had a message. Now I only say 'fight the damned socialists'. I do not believe in this brave new world.

1944[2]

Critics

I have derived continued benefit from criticism at all periods
of my life and I do not remember any time when I was ever
short of it.

1914[1]

You see these microphones? They have been placed on our
tables by the British Broadcasting Corporation ... We can
picture Sir John Reith, with the perspiration mantling on his
lofty brow, with his hand on the control switch, wondering, as
I utter every word, whether it will not be his duty to protect his
innocent subscribers from some irreverent thing I might say
about Mr Gandhi, or about the Bolsheviks, or even about our
peripatetic Prime Minister.

1933[2] *Sir John Reith, managing director of the BBC, was no admirer.*

Because half-a-dozen grasshoppers under a fern make the field
ring with their importunate chink, whilst thousands of great
cattle repose beneath the shadow of the British oak, chew the
cud and are silent, pray do not imagine that those who make
the noise are the only inhabitants of the field, that of course
they are many in number; or that, after all, they are other than
the little shrivelled, meagre, hopping, though loud and
troublesome insects of the hour.

1939[3]

Deafness

Why do you stop reading? Don't you know that water is a
conductor of sound?

1952[1] *In his bath, listening to secret reports being read by Sir Leslie Hollis,
Churchill suddenly submerged.*

WSC: Who's that speaking?
  Julian Amery: Braine.
  WSC: James?

Amery: No! Braine.
WSC: Drain. He can't be called Drain. Nobody's called Drain.
Amery wrote 'Braine' on the back of an order paper.
WSC: Ah! I see. Is he well named?
1956[2]

Death (see also 'Afterlife')
Although always prepared for martyrdom, I preferred that it
should be postponed.
1930[1]

I am ready to meet my Maker. Whether my Maker is prepared
for the great ordeal of meeting me is another matter.
1949[2]

I am informed from many quarters that a rumour has been put
about that I died this morning. This is quite untrue.
1951[3]

Dress
How should I not be out at elbows when my father is out of
office?
1894 *When reproved for returning home from Harrow with a torn jacket.*

Dukedom
Duke of Bardogs would sound well, and Randolph could be
Marquess of Chartwell.
1947[1] *Churchill acquired 120-acre Bardogs Farm in 1947.*

I should have to be the Duke of Chartwell, and Randolph
would be the Marquess of Toodledo.
1952[2]

First, what could I be Duke of? Secondly even if I were Duke of Westerham, what would Randolph be? He could only be Marquess of Puddledock Lane, which is the only other possession I have apart from Chartwell. And thirdly, and quite seriously, I wish to die in the House of Commons as Winston Churchill.

1955[3]

Eating words

In the course of my life I have often had to eat my words, and I must confess that I have always found it a wholesome diet.

circa 1940s

Elections

[1899] Everyone threw the blame on me. I have noticed that they nearly always do.

1930[1]

[1922] In a twinkling of an eye I found myself without an office, without a seat, without a party, and without an appendix.

1931[2] *WSC was struck by appendicitis while losing an election.*

[1945]; Clementine Churchill: 'It may well be a blessing in disguise.'

WSC: At the moment it seems quite effectively disguised.

1945[3]

[1951] ... this is the first occasion when I have addressed this assembly here as Prime Minister. The explanation is convincing. When I should have come here as Prime Minister the Guildhall was blown up, and before it was repaired I was blown out!

1951[4]

Examinations

These examinations were a great trial to me ... I should have liked to be asked to say what I knew. They always tried to ask what I did not know.

1930[1]

I wrote my name at the top of the page. I wrote down the number of the question 'I'. After much reflection I put a bracket round it thus '(I)'. But thereafter I could not think of anything connected with it that was either relevant or true. Incidentally there arrived from nowhere in particular a blot and several smudges.

1930[2] *WSC's professed failure in his Latin exam is almost certainly myth; Harrow researchers have never found the subject exam paper.*

I am surprised that in my later life I should have become so experienced in taking degrees, when, as a schoolboy I was so bad at passing examinations. In fact one might almost say that no one ever passed so few examinations and received so many degrees.

1946[3]

Family

Where does the family start? It starts with a young man falling in love with a girl. No superior alternative has yet been found!

1950

Farming

I am going to make my farm pay, whatever it costs.

1926

Fate

... of course one only has to look at Nature and see how very little store she sets by life. Its sanctity is entirely a human idea. You may think of a beautiful butterfly 12 million feathers on his wings, 16,000 lenses in his eye a mouthful for a bird. Let us laugh at Fate. It might please her.

1898[1]

Si une bombe tombe sur la maison, nous mourrons ensemble comme deux braves gens! [If a bomb falls on this building, we will die nobly together.]

1940[2] *WSC to the BBC's Jacques Duchesne, who remarked that there did not seem much security at Number Ten. WSC burst out laughing.*

I will get on the plane and take my pill and I will wake up either in Bermuda or in heaven. Unless one of you gentlemen has another fate in mind for me.

1953[3]

Fitness and health

Gen. Montgomery: I neither drink nor smoke and I am 100 percent fit.

WSC: I drink and smoke and I am 200 percent fit.

1942[1] *Reported exchange when Churchill appointed Montgomery commander of the Eighth Army.*

Sir Charles has been a terrible anxiety to us the whole time, but I hope we'll get him through.

[After holding forth lengthily on medicine and psychology]

… My God! I do have to work hard to teach that chap his job!

1942[2] *WSC's doctor, Sir Charles Moran (later Lord Moran), fell ill with an upset stomach.*

I get my exercise serving as pall-bearer to my many friends who exercised all their lives.

circa 1950s[3]

Food Rationing

WSC: Not a bad meal, not a bad meal ...

Minister of Food: But these are not rations for a meal or for a day. They are for a *week*.

WSC: A week! Then the people are starving. It must be remedied.

circa 1951 *Wartime rationing had been continued under the postwar Labour government. Churchill's 1951 administration eventually ended it.*

Foresight

[I strive for ...] the ability to foretell what is going to happen tomorrow, next week, next month, and next year – and to have the ability afterwards to explain why it didn't happen.

1902

Golf

Like chasing a quinine pill around a cow pasture.

circa 1915 *WSC played golf indifferently from circa 1910 to the 1920s.*

Horses

No hour of life is lost that is spent in the saddle. Young men have often been ruined through owning horses, or through backing horses, but never through riding them; unless of course they break their necks, which, taken at a gallop, is a very good death to die.

1930[1]

I told him this is a very big race and if he won it he would never have to run again but spend the rest of his life in agreeable female company. Colonist II did not keep his mind on the race.

1949[2] *His best race horse, Colonist II, had lost a race ...*

To stud? And have it said that the Prime Minister of Great Britain is living off the immoral earnings of a horse?

circa 1949[3] *It was suggested that WSC put Colonist II out to stud.*

Improvising

Harold Macmillan: What are you doing, Prime Minister?
  WSC: Rehearsing my impromptu witticisms.

circa 1941–54 *A less amusing version is in Macmillan 1969, 496:*
'Preparing improvisations! Very hard work!'

Inconsistency

My views are a harmonious process which keeps them in
relation to the current movements of events.

1952

Influenza

It was an English bug which I took abroad with me, and no
blame rests on the otherwise misguided continent of Europe.

1932

Interfering

You mean like a great blue-bottle buzzing over a huge cowpat!

1942 *Eden suggested WSC should not go and interfere with commanders in*
the Middle East. WSC went and interfered greatly: Auchinleck was
dismissed.

Interrupting

All the years that I have been in the House I have always said
to myself one thing: 'Do not interrupt', and I have never been
able to keep to that resolution.

1935[1]

Randolph, do not interrupt me while I'm interrupting!

circa 1930s[2] *WSC to his son.*

Knighthood

Now Clemmie will have to be a lady at last.

1953 *WSC had been offered a Knighthood of the Garter.*

Life (see also 'Fate')

I'm glad I've not to live my life over again. There is a dreadful degradation of standards.

1950

Mathematics

... the figures were tied into all sorts of tangles and did things to one another which it was extremely difficult to forecast with complete accuracy. You had to say what they did each time they were tied up together ... In some cases these figures got into debt with one another: you had to borrow one or carry one, and afterwards you had to pay back the one you had borrowed.

1930[1]

We were arrived in an 'Alice-in-Wonderland' world, at the portals of which stood 'A Quadratic Equation'. This with a strange grimace pointed the way to the Theory of Indices, which again handed on the intruder to the full rigours of the Binomial Theorem. Further dim chambers lighted by sullen, sulphurous fires were reputed to contain a dragon called the 'Differential Calculus'. But this monster was beyond the bounds appointed by the Civil Service Commissioners who regulated this stage of Pilgrim's heavy journey. We turned aside not indeed to the uplands of the Delectable Mountains, but into a strange corridor of things like anagrams and acrostics called Sines, Cosines and Tangents. Apparently they were very important, especially when multiplied by each other, or by themselves! ... I have never met any of these creatures since.

1930[2]

I had a feeling once about Mathematics, that I saw it all – Depth beyond Depth was revealed to me – the Byss and the Abyss. I saw, as one might see the transit of Venus – or even the Lord Mayor's Show, a quantity passing through infinity and changing its sign from plus to minus. I saw exactly how it happened and why the tergiversation was inevitable: and how the one step involved all the others. It was like politics. But it was after dinner and I let it go!

1930[3]

Meals and Courses

This hotel is a great trial to me. Yesterday morning I had half-eaten a kipper when a huge maggot crept out & flashed his teeth at me! Today I could find nothing nourishing for lunch but pancakes. Such are the trials wh[ich] great & good men endure in the service of their country!

1909[1] *WSC to his wife.*

American meals nearly always start with a large slice of melon or grapefruit accompanied by iced water. This is surely a somewhat austere welcome for a hungry man at the midday or evening meal. Dessert, in my view, should be eaten at the end of the meal, not at the beginning. The influence of American customs is now so all-pervading, that during the last few years I have noticed this habit creeping into England. It should be strongly repulsed.

1933[2]

That is indeed a magnificent fish: I must 'have some of him' … No! No! I will have meat. Carnivores will win this war!

circa 1940s[3]

Almost all the food faddists I have ever known, nut-eaters and the like, have died young after a long period of senile decay …

1940[4] *WSC to Minister of Food, Lord Woolton.*

… these miserable mice [quail] should never have been removed from Tutankhamen's tomb!

1942[5]

Ten demerits! You should know no gentleman eats ham sandwiches without mustard.

1942[6]

Stilton and port are like man and wife. They should never be separated. 'Whom God has joined together, let no man put asunder.' No – nor woman either.

1946[7]

Pray take away this pudding. It has no theme.

circa 1946–51[8] *Remark at one of WSC's lunches for the Shadow Cabinet while Parliament was sitting.*

Painting

Like a sea-beast fished up from the depths, or a diver too suddenly hoisted, my veins threatened to burst from the fall in pressure … And then it was that the Muse of Painting came to my rescue – out of charity and out of chivalry, because after all she had nothing to do with me – and said, 'Are these toys any good to you? They amuse some people.'

1921[1]

… very gingerly I mixed a little blue paint on the palette with a very small brush, and then with infinite precaution made a mark about as big as a bean upon the affronted snow-white shield. It was a challenge, a deliberate challenge; but so subdued, so halting, indeed so cataleptic, that it deserved no response. At that moment the loud approaching sound of a motor-car was heard in the drive. From this chariot there stepped swiftly and lightly none other than the gifted wife of Sir John Lavery. 'Painting! But what are you hesitating about? Let me have a brush, the big one.' Splash into the turpentine, wallop into the blue and the white, frantic flourish on the palette, clean no longer, and then several large, fierce strokes and slashes of blue on the absolutely cowering canvas. Anyone could see that it could not hit back. No evil fate avenged the jaunty violence. The canvas grinned in helplessness before me. The spell was broken. The sickly inhibitions rolled away. I seized the largest brush and fell upon my victim with berserk fury. I have never felt any awe of a canvas since.

1921[2]

I cannot pretend to feel impartial about the colours. I rejoice with the brilliant ones, and am genuinely sorry for the poor browns. When I get to heaven I mean to spend a considerable portion of my first million years in painting, and so get to the bottom of the subject.

1922[3]

Fetch me associate and fraternal bottles to form a bodyguard to this majestic container!

circa 1930s[4] *Churchill gave the name 'Bottlescape' to one of his famous still life paintings. One Christmas, he was given a huge bottle of brandy; he sent the children scurrying around Chartwell to find other bottles to paint with it.*

... a tree doesn't complain that I haven't done it justice.

circa 1930s[5]

Can't we get rid of this vast white space? ... I always survey the whole scene with greater clarity if I attack the white areas first and afterwards concentrate on the pockets of resistance.

1933[6] *WSC's nephew Johnnie was painting murals in the garden loggia at Chartwell.*

If the finished product looks like a work of art, then it *is* a work of art.

1946[7] *WSC's retort when his detective, observing him projecting a magic lantern image of an unfinished scene on to a canvas to guide his brushstrokes, said, 'Looks a bit like cheating.'*

Predestination

WSC: Hadn't you better stay under cover?

Lord Beaverbrook: Wa'al, I am a Presbyterian and believe in Predestination.

WSC: Yes, but does Hitler?

1940 *Desmond Morton to Leo Amery. Lord Beaverbrook was leaving Number Ten when anti-aircraft firing began.*

Prodding

I am certainly not one of those who need to be prodded. In fact, if anything, I am a prod.

1942

Prophesying

… I always avoid prophesying beforehand, because it is much better policy to prophesy after the event has already taken place.

1943

Religion

I don't think much of God. He hasn't put enough in the pool.

1907[1]

[Evidence that God exists] is the existence of Lenin and Trotsky, for whom a hell [is] needed.

1929[2]

I accumulated in those years [as a boy] so fine a surplus in the Bank of Observance that I have been drawing confidently upon it ever since. Weddings, christenings and funerals have brought in a steady annual income, and I have never made too close enquiries about the state of my account. It might well even be that I should find an overdraft.

1930[3]

I am glad I went. It's the first time my mind has been at rest for a long time. Besides, I like singing hymns.

1941[4] *Roosevelt took WSC with him to a Methodist church, saying: 'It's good for Winston to sing hymns with the Methodies.'*

I wouldn't have [God's] job for anything. Mine is hard enough, but His is much more difficult. And – hmph – He can't even resign.

1949[5]

I am not a pillar of the church but a buttress – I support it from the outside.

circa 1954[6]

Retirement

I refuse to be exhibited like a prize bull whose chief attraction is its past prowess.

1945[1]

My dear Edward, you can tell your colleagues that one of the unalterable rules of my life is never to leave the pub until closing time.

circa 1947[2] *Lord Halifax had suggested in private, on behalf of many Tories, that WSC should resign as Leader of the Opposition.*

[Reporter: 'Do you have any thoughts of retiring?'] Not until I am a great deal worse and the Empire a great deal better.

1953[3]

I feel like an aeroplane at the end of its flight, in the dusk, with the petrol running out, in search of a safe landing.

1954[4] *WSC to R.A. Butler.*

Reward poster

I think you might have gone as high as fifty pounds without an over-estimate of the value of the prize – if living!

1908 *WSC to Mr de Haas, the police officer who offered £25 reward for the recapture of Churchill dead or alive after his escape from the Boer prison in 1899.*

Rudeness

WSC: You were very rude to me, you know.

Nurse Roy Howells: Yes, but you were rude too.

WSC replied 'with just a hint of a smile': Yes, but I am a great man.

circa 1958

Running

Please see *The Times* of February 4. Is it really true that a seven-mile cross-country run is enforced upon all in this division, from generals to privates? Does the Army Council think this a good idea? It looks to me rather excessive. A colonel or general ought not to exhaust himself in trying to compete with young boys running across country seven miles at a time. Who is the general of this division and does he run the seven miles himself? If so, he may be more useful for football than war. Could Napoleon have run seven miles across country at Austerlitz? Perhaps it was the other fellow he made run.

1941 *It is broadly understood that the general was Montgomery, a fitness proponent. (See Fitness and health.)*

Self-expression

We are all worms. But I do believe that I am a glow-worm.

1906[1]

His Excellency, after the health of the Queen Empress had been drunk and dinner was over, was good enough to ask my opinion upon several matters, and considering the magnificent character of his hospitality, I thought it would be unbecoming in me not to reply fully ... There were indeed moments when he seemed willing to impart his own views; but I thought it would be ungracious to put him to so much trouble; and he very readily subsided.

1930[2] *An 1895 conversation with Lord Sandhurst, Governor of Bombay; Winston was a subaltern aged twenty-one.*

I have in my life concentrated more on self-expression than on self-denial.

1953[3]

Servants

WSC: My dear Maxine, do you realise I have come all the way from London without my man?

Maxine Elliott, for once getting the last word: Winston, how terribly brave of you.

circa 1939

Sex

Tobacco is bad for love; but old age is worse.

1951[1]

Sex was not born till protoplasm – or protozoa if you prefer – divided itself. But for this split the sexes would not have had all the fun of coming together again.

1954[2]

Skin

I have a very delicate and sensitive cuticle which demands the finest covering. Look at the texture of my cuticle – feel it [uncovering his forearm by rolling up his sleeve]. I have a cuticle without a blemish – except on one small portion of my anatomy where I sacrificed a piece of skin to accommodate a wounded brother-officer on my way back from the Sudan campaign.

circa 1908

Staphylococcus

The bug seems to have caught my truculence. This is its finest hour.

1946

Suicide

If one is to be hanged, it should be for a capital offence. It is never necessary to commit suicide, especially when you may live to regret it.

circa 1953 *A relatively minor parliamentary Bill seemed likely to cause the government, which had a very small majority, to be defeated.*

Thought

My dear young man, thought is the most dangerous process known to man.

undated *WSC to Lord Home, who had said he would like a little time to think over a complicated issue of policy.*

Trinity

Moi, je suis un frère aîné de la Trinité.

1914[1] *In Antwerp to rally the city's defenders, WSC wore the uniform of an Elder Brother of Trinity House (Britain's lighthouse authority), explaining to a confused Belgian, who thought WSC considered himself divine.*

It is very nice of them [Cambridge]. And I ought certainly to be pleased. After all, it will put me alongside the Trinity.

1958[2] *Cambridge University had accepted the new Churchill College; Trinity College is part of Cambridge.*

Unpunctuality

I realised that I must be upon my best behaviour: punctual, subdued, reserved, in short display all the qualities with which I am least endowed.

1930 *Before an 1896 dinner for the Prince of Wales.*

Volubility
Asking me not to make a speech is like asking a centipede to get along and not put a foot on the ground.
1940

Writing
I earned my livelihood by dictating articles which had a wide circulation ... I lived in fact from mouth to hand.
1948

Appendix

Listed below are the most popular witticisms incorrectly ascribed to Churchill. Many remarks which he *did* use actually originated with others, such as 'Democracy is the worst system, except for all the other systems.' Ribald quotations are also often ascribed to Churchill, but he was not given to smutty remarks, and nearly always treated the opposite sex with Victorian courtesy.

Attlee, Clement
An empty car drew up and Clement Attlee got out ... Attlee is a sheep in sheep's clothing.
Neither has attribution. The Quote Verifier editor Ralph Keyes wrote the editor: 'British quote researcher Nigel Rees thought the comment might have originated with newspaper columnist J. B. Morton in the 1930s.'

Balfour, Arthur
If you wanted nothing done, Arthur Balfour was the best man for the task. There was no one equal to him.
Allegedly said to Lloyd George; no attribution.

Beer bottles
... we shall fight in the fields and in the streets, we shall fight in the hills ... And we will hit them over the heads with beer bottles, which is about all we have got to work with ...
1940 *Taylor says the latter part of this was heard by a clergyman present at the studio ... Sir John Colville, who was present, did not hear it.*

Birth
Although present on that occasion I have no clear recollection of the events leading up to it.
Unattributed by Manchester, or anyone else.

Bull in a China Shop

He is the only bull I know who carries his china shop with him.

Allegedly said about John Foster Dulles, but not tracked anywhere in Churchill's 15 million published words.

Cigars and women

Smoking cigars is like falling in love; first you are attracted to its shape; you stay for its flavour; and you must always remember never, never let the flame go out.

2005 *Hearsay attributed to Randolph Churchill.*

Common language

Britain and America are two nations divided by a common language.

1940s *Closest we have is Ralph Keyes in* The Quote Verifier, *from Oscar Wilde's 'The Canterville Ghost' (1887): 'We have really everything in common with America nowadays, except, of course, language.'*

Cross of Lorraine

The heaviest cross I have to bear is the Cross of Lorraine.

1943 *A reference to de Gaulle, but no attribution is found; sometimes thought to have been said by General Edward Louis Spears, head of the British mission to France, 1940–42.*

Democracy

The best argument against Democracy is a five minute conversation with the average voter.

Commonly quoted, but no attribution.

… democracy is the worst form of Government except for all those other forms that have been tried from time to time …

1947[1] *These are Churchill's words, but preceded with 'as has been said …' Clearly, he was not the originator.*

Dinner, wine and women

Well, dinner would have been splendid if the wine had been as cold as the soup, the beef as rare as the service, the brandy as old as the fish, and the maid as willing as the Duchess.

Certainly manufactured. WSC would not have stayed for the second course of such a meal, and his remarks about women were, with rare exceptions, gallant.

Dukes

… a fully equipped duke costs as much to keep as two dreadnoughts; and dukes are just as great a terror and they last longer.

1909 *The speaker was WSC's ally in the campaign to reform the House of Lords, David Lloyd George.*

Feet first

Not feet-first, please!

1962 *Supposedly said to a stretcher-bearer carrying him to an ambulance after breaking his leg at Monte Carlo; no attribution.*

Golf

A curious sport whose object is to put a very small ball in a very small hole with implements ill-designed for the purpose.

circa 1915 *Incorrectly footnoted in Manchester; unattributed.*

Hell

If you're going through hell, keep going.

All over the internet but without attribution.

Ingratitude

Ingratitude towards their great men is the mark of strong peoples.

1949 *WSC credited Plutarch with this remark. He was commenting on the discarding of the French WW1 leader Georges Clemenceau.*

Jaw, jaw

Jaw, jaw is better than war, war.

1954 Sir Martin Gilbert told Finest Hour *that Churchill actually said, 'Meeting jaw to jaw is better than war.' Four years later, during a visit to Australia, Harold Macmillan said, 'Jaw, jaw is better than war, war.'*

Kissing and climbing

The most difficult things for a man to do are to climb a wall leaning towards you, and to kiss a girl leaning away from you.
Commonly ascribed, but nowhere in the canon.

Liberal and conservative

If a man is not liberal in youth he has no heart. If he is not conservative when older he has no brain.
All over the internet, but not in the canon.

Lies

There are a terrible lot of lies going about the world, and the worst of it is that half of them are true.
1906 Churchill explained that this was said by a 'witty Irishman'.

Living and life

You make a living by what you get; you make a life by what you give.
Reiterated in many sources including a 2005 TV ad by Lockheed Martin. An old saw put in Churchill's mouth.

Marx Brothers

You are my fifth favourite actor. The first four are the Marx Brothers.
Reported in at least one Churchill quotations book, but this comment is not established as ever being uttered.

Monarchy, constitutional

Well may it be said, well was it said, that the prerogatives of the Crown have become the privileges of the people.

1945 Churchill's first nine words (usually omitted in this quotation) show that he was quoting an earlier source.

Montgomery, Bernard

In defeat, indomitable; in victory, insufferable. [Or:] Indomitable in retreat, invincible in advance, insufferable in victory.

Widely bruited about, but nowhere in the canon.

Naval tradition

It's nothing but rum, buggery [sometimes 'sodomy'] and the lash.

circa 1914–15 Specifically denied by WSC. 'Compare "Rum, bum, and bacca" and "Ashore it's wine women and song, aboard it's rum, bum and concertina", naval catchphrases dating from the nineteenth century' – Oxford Dictionary of Quotations.

Oats and sage

The young sow wild oats, the old grow sage.

Constantly ascribed to Churchill, it tracks back to 'An Adage', by Henry James Byron (1835–84).

Poison in your coffee

Nancy Astor: If I were married to you, I'd put poison in your coffee.

WSC: If I were married to you, I'd drink it.

*circa 1912 Fred Shapiro (*Yale Book of Quotations*) tracks this to a joke line in the* Chicago Tribune *of 3 January 1900, but it was likely repeated to Astor by Churchill's best friend F. E. Smith, Lord Birkenhead.*

Prepositions

This is the kind of tedious [or 'pedantic'] nonsense up with which I will not put.

1944 Originally attributed to WSC in The New York Times *and* Chicago Tribune, *28 February 1944. In 1942, however,* The Wall Street Journal *ascribed it to an unnamed memorandum writer.*

Simple tastes

I am a man of simple tastes – I am quite easily satisfied with the best of everything.

1930s *Possibly said about Churchill by F. E. Smith, this originates in Shaw's 1905 play* Major Barbara *(act 1, scene 1), where Lady Britomart says: 'I know your quiet, simple, refined, poetic people like Adolphus – quite content with the best of everything!'*

Speeches, long vs short

I am going to make a long speech today; I haven't had time to prepare a short one.

No Churchill attribution. In 1656, Blaise Pascal wrote to a friend: 'I have only made this letter rather long because I have not had time to make it shorter.'

Success

Success is not final, failure is not fatal: it is the courage to continue that counts.

No Churchill source is found. Ascribed to Jules Ellinger by Quotationsbook.com, but no attribution is cited.

Urinal humour

Churchill, seeing Attlee approach the House of Commons urinal, shuffled a few feet away. Attlee: 'A bit stand-offish today, are we, Winston?'

  WSC: Every time you socialists see something big, you want to nationalise it.

circa 1948 *Recorded by Manchester and others, but not attributed. Verdict: apocryphal Churchill.*

Virtues and vices

He has all the virtues I dislike and none of the vices I admire.

Allegedly said about Stafford Cripps or Edwin Scrymgeour; no evidence in the canon.

Bibliography

Any quotation not annotated except by date is from the Parliamentary Debates (Hansard) as transcribed the *Complete Speeches* ('CS', see below). All other quotations are identified by page numbers. Works by Churchill himself are conveyed by title words or acronyms, e.g. 'Crisis' for *The World Crisis*, 'MEL' for *My Early Life*. Works by other authors are identified by the author's name and, if he or she wrote more than one work, part of the title, e.g. 'Gilbert, Life, 89'.

Books by Winston S. Churchill

Arms and the Covenant. London: George G. Harrap & Co., 1938.

Blood, Sweat and Tears. Toronto: McClelland & Stewart, 1941. Published in London as *Into Battle*, 1941.

The Boer War. Combining *London to Ladysmith via Pretoria* and *Ian Hamilton's March*. London: Leo Cooper, 1989.

Collected Essays of Sir Winston Churchill. 4 vols. London: Library of Imperial History, 1975.

The Dawn of Liberation. London: Cassell, 1945.

The Dream. Text is from the official biography (Official Biography), vol. VIII. First published in *The Daily Telegraph*, 1966. First published in volume form by The Churchill Literary Foundation (Churchill Centre), 1987.

The End of the Beginning. Boston: Little Brown & Co., 1943.

Europe Unite: Speeches 1947 & 1948. London: Cassell, 1950.

Great Contemporaries. Revised and extended edition. London: Leo Cooper, 1990. First published 1937.

A History of the English-Speaking Peoples. 4 vols. New York: Dodd, Mead & Co., 1956–58.

Ian Hamilton's March. London: Longmans Green, 1900.

In the Balance: Speeches 1949 & 1950. London: Cassell, 1951.

India. Hopkinton, N.H.: Dragonwyck Publishing Inc., 1990. First published 1931.

Liberalism and the Social Problem. Reprinted in *The Collected Works of Sir Winston Churchill*. Vol. VII, *Early Speeches*. London: Library of Imperial History, 1974. First published 1910.

London to Ladysmith via Pretoria. London: Longmans Green, 1900.

Lord Randolph Churchill. London: Macmillan, 1907. First published in 2 vols., 1906.

Marlborough: His Life and Times. 4 vols. London: Sphere Books, 1967. First published 1933–38.

Mr. Brodrick's Army. Sacramento: The Churchilliana Co., 1977. Reset edition. First published 1903.

My Early Life: A Roving Commission. London: Thornton Butterworth, 1930.

Onwards to Victory. London: Cassell, 1944.

The People's Rights. London: Jonathan Cape, 1970. First published 1910.

The River War: An Historical Account of the Reconquest of the Soudan. 2 vols. London: Longmans, Green, 1899.

Savrola: A Tale of the Revolution in Laurania. London: Leo Cooper, 1990. First published 1899.

The Second World War. 6 vols. London: Cassell, 1948–54.

Secret Session Speeches. London: Cassell, 1946.

The Sinews of Peace: Post-War Speeches. London: Cassell, 1948.

Stemming the Tide: Speeches 1951 & 1952. London: Cassell, 1953.

Step by Step 1936–1939. London: Odhams, 1947. First published 1939.

The Story of the Malakand Field Force 1897. London: Leo Cooper, 1989. First published 1898.

Thoughts and Adventures. London: Leo Cooper, 1990. First published 1932.

The Unrelenting Struggle. Boston: Little Brown & Co., 1942.

The Unwritten Alliance: Speeches 1953–1959. London: Cassell, 1961.

Victory. London: Cassell, 1946.

Winston S. Churchill: His Complete Speeches 1897–1963, edited by Sir Robert Rhodes James, 8 vols., New York: Bowker, 1974.

The World Crisis. 5 vols. in 6 parts. London: Thornton Butterworth, 1923–31.

The Official Biography (Official Biography)

Winston S. Churchill, by Randolph S. Churchill (vols. I–II) and Sir Martin Gilbert (vols. III–VIII), together with the accompanying Companion (Document) Volumes, was published between 1967 and 1988 by Heinemann, London, and Houghton Mifflin,

Boston. Three additional Companion Volumes (*The Churchill War Papers*) were published between 1993 and 2000 by Heinemann and W. W. Norton (New York). In 2006, the complete work began to be reprinted, eventually to include additional Companion Volumes provided by Gilbert, by the Hillsdale College Press, Hillsdale, Michigan. Page references throughout are to the Heinemann editions.

Official Biography, I. *Youth 1874–1900*. Published 1966.

Official Biography, II. *Young Statesman 1901–1911*. Published 1967.

Official Biography, III. *The Challenge of War 1914–1916*. Published 1971.

Official Biography, IV. *The Stricken World 1917–1922*. Published 1975.

Official Biography, V. *The Prophet of Truth 1922–1929*. Published 1976.

Official Biography, VI. *Finest Hour 1939–1941*. Published 1983.

Official Biography, VII. *Road to Victory 1941–1945*. Published 1986.

Official Biography, VIII. *Never Despair 1945–1965*. Published 1988.

Official Biography, CV1/1: *Companion Volume I, Part 1 1874–1896*. Published 1967.

Official Biography, CV1/2: *Companion Volume I, Part 2 1896–1900*. Published 1967.

Official Biography, CV2/1: *Companion Volume II, Part 1 1901–1907*. Published 1969.

Official Biography, CV2/2: *Companion Volume II, Part 2 1907–1911*. Published 1969.

Official Biography, CV2/3: *Companion Volume II, Part 3 1911–1914*. Published 1969.

Official Biography, CV3/1: *Companion Volume III, Part 1: Documents, July 1914–April 1915*. Published 1972.

Official Biography, CV3/2: *Companion Volume III, Part 2: Documents, May 1915–December 1916*. Published 1972.

Official Biography, CV4/1: *Companion Volume IV, Part 1: Documents, January 1917–June 1919*. Published 1977.

Official Biography, CV4/2: *Companion Volume IV, Part 2: Documents, July 1919–March 1921*. Published 1977.

Official Biography, CV4/3: *Companion Volume IV, Part 3: Documents, April 1921–November 1922*. Published 1977.

Official Biography, CV5/1: *Companion Volume V, Part 1: Documents, The Exchequer Years 1922–1929*. Published 1979.

Official Biography, CV5/2: *Companion Volume V, Part 2: Documents, The Wilderness Years 1929–1935*. Published 1981.

Official Biography, CV5/3: *Companion Volume V, Part 3: Documents: The Coming of War 1936–1939*. Published 1982.

Official Biography, CV6/1: *The Churchill War Papers, Volume I: At the Admiralty, September 1939–May 1940*. Published 1993.

Official Biography, CV6/2: *The Churchill War Papers, Volume II: Never Surrender, May 1940–December 1940*. Published 1994.

Official Biography, CV6/3: *The Churchill War Papers, Volume III: The Ever-Widening War, 1941*. Published 2000.

Books by Other Authors

For authors of multiple titles, their works are stated in chronological order of publication.

Adler, Bill, ed. *The Churchill Wit*. New York: Coward-McCann, 1965.

Amery, Julian. *Approach March*. London: Hutchinson, 1973.

Balsan, Consuelo. *The Glitter and the Gold*. London: Heinemann, 1953.

Barnes, J. and Nicholson, D., editors. *The Empire at Bay: The Leo Amery Diaries 1929–1945*. London: Hutchinson, 1988.

BBC, editors. *Winston Churchill: Memories and Tributes Broadcast by the BBC*. London: BBC, 1965.

Beaverbrook, Max. *Politicians and the War 1914–1916*. London: Thornton Butterworth, 1928.

_____. *The Decline and Fall of Lloyd George*. London: Collins, 1963.

Ben-Moshe, Tuvla. *Churchill: Strategy and History*. Boulder, Colorado: Lynne Rienner Publishers, 1992.

Birkenhead, Earl of. *The Life of Lord Halifax*. Boston: Houghton Mifflin, 1966.

Bonham Carter, Violet. *Winston Churchill: An Intimate Portrait*. New York: Harcourt Brace & World, 1965.

Boothby, Robert. *Recollections of a Rebel*. London: Hutchinson, 1978.

Boyle, Andrew. *Poor, Dear Brendan: The Quest for Brendan Bracken*. London: Hutchinson, 1974.

Boyle, Peter. *The Churchill-Eisenhower Correspondence 1953–1955*. Chapel Hill, N.C.: University of North Carolina Press, 1990.

Broad, Lewis. *Winston Churchill*. Revised and extended edition. London: Hutchinson, 1945.

Bryant, Arthur. *The Turn of the Tide 1939–1943*. New York: Doubleday & Co., 1957.

Bryant, Arthur. *Triumph in the West 1943–1946*. London: Collins, 1959.

Cadogan, Alexander (ed. David Dilks). *The Diaries of Sir Alexander Cadogan OM, 1938–1945*. London: Cassell, 1971.

Cawthorne, Graham. *The Churchill Legend: An Anthology*. London: Cleaver-Hume Press, n.d. [1965].

Channon, Henry. *Chips: The Diaries of Sir Henry Channon*. London: Weidenfeld & Nicholson, 1967.

Chaplin, E.D.W. *Winston Churchill at Harrow*. Harrow, Middlesex: The Harrow Bookshop, n.d. [1941].

Charmley, John. *Churchill: The End of Glory*. London: Hodder & Stoughton, 1993.

Chisholme, Anne and Davie, Michael. *Beaverbrook: A Life*. London: Hutchinson, 1992.

Churchill, John Spencer. *Crowded Canvas*. London: Odhams, 1961.

Colville, John. *Footprints in Time: Memories*. London: Collins, 1976.

_____. *The Fringes of Power: Downing Street Diaries 1940–1955*. 2 vols. Sevenoaks, Kent: Sceptre Publishing, 1986–7.

Cowles, Virginia. *Winston Churchill: The Era And The Man*. London: Hamish Hamilton, 1953.

Dalton, Hugh. 'Winston: A Memoir.' *New Statesman*, April 1965.

Deakin, F.W. *Churchill the Historian*. Zurich: Fondation Suisse Winston Churchill, 1970.

Dilks, David. 'Allied Leadership in the Second World War: Churchill.' *Survey,* no. 1 /2, Winter–Spring 1975.

_____. *The Great Dominion; Winston Churchill in Canada 1900–1954*. Toronto: Thomas Allen, 2005.

Donaldson, Frances. *Edward VIII: A Biography of the Duke of Windsor*. Philadelphia: Lippincott, 1974.

Eade, Charles, ed. *Churchill by His Contemporaries*. London: Hutchinson, 1953.

Eden, Sir Anthony. *The Eden Memoirs: The Reckoning*. London: Cassell, 1965.

'Ephesian' (Roberts, C. Bechofer). *Winston Churchill*. Third Edition. London: George Newnes, 1936. First published 1927.

Fishman, Jack. *My Darling Clementine*. New York: McKay, 1963.

Gilbert, Martin. *Churchill: The Wilderness Years*. Boston: Houghton Mifflin, 1982.

_____. *Churchill: A Life*. London: Heinemann, 1991.

_____. *In Search of Churchill*. London: HarperCollins, 1994.

Graebner, Walter. *My Dear Mr Churchill*. London: Michael Joseph, 1965.

Gretton. *Former Naval Person*. London: Cassell, 1968.

Guedalla, Philip. *Mr Churchill: A Portrait*. London: Hodder & Stoughton, 1941.

Halle, Kay. *Irrepressible Churchill*. Cleveland: World, 1966.

_____. *Winston Churchill on America and Britain: A Selection of his Thoughts on Anglo-American Relations*. New York: Walker, 1970.

Hamblin, Grace. 'Chartwell Memories.' *Proceedings of the International Churchill Society, 1987*. Hopkinton, N.H.: International Churchill Society, 1989.

Hart-Davis, D. (ed) *King's Counsellor*. London: Weidenfeld & Nicholson, 2006.

Hassall, Christopher. *Edward Marsh*. London: Longmans Green & Co., 1959.

Home, Alec Douglas. *The Way the Wind Blows*. London: Collins, 1976.

_____. *Letters to a Grandson*. London: Collins, 1983.

Howells, Roy. *Simply Churchill*. London: Robert Hale, 1965.

Ismay, Lord. *Memoirs of General the Lord Ismay*. London: Heinemann, 1960.

Kennedy, John. *The Business of War: The War Narrative of Major-General Sir John Kennedy*. London: Hutchinson, 1957.

Keyes, Ralph. *The Quote Verifier*. New York: St Martin's Griffin, 2006.

Kersaudy, François. *Churchill and de Gaulle*. New York: Athenaeum, 1982.

Leasor, James. *War at the Top*. London: Michael Joseph, 1959.

Longford, Elizabeth. *Winston Churchill*. London: Sidgwick & Jackson, 1974.

Lowenheim. *Roosevelt and Churchill: Their Secret Wartime Correspondence*. New York: Saturday Review Press/E.P. Dutton & Co., 1975.

Lyttleton, Oliver. *Memoirs of Lord Chandos*. London: The Bodley Head, 1962.

MacCallum Scott. *Winston Churchill*. London: Methuen, 1905.

MacDonald, Malcolm. *Titans and Others*. London: Collins, 1972.

Maclean, Sir Fitzroy. 'Humanity – A Churchillian Characteristic.' *Proceedings of the International Churchill Society, 1987*. Hopkinton, N.H.: International Churchill Society, 1989.

Macmillan, Harold. *The Blast of War 1939–1945*. London: Macmillan, 1968.

_____. *Tides of Fortune 1945–1955*. London: Macmillan, 1969.

Manchester, William. *The Last Lion: Winston Spencer Churchill*. Vol. 1 *Visions of Glory 1874–1932*. Boston: Little Brown, 1983. Vol. 2. *Alone 1932–1940*. Boston: Little Brown, 1988.

Marchant, Sir James, ed. *Winston Spencer Churchill: Servant of Crown and Commonwealth*. London: Cassell, 1954.

Marsh, Edward. *A Number of People.* London: Heinemann, 1939.

Martin, Hugh. *Battle: The Life Story of the Rt. Hon. Winston S. Churchill.* London: Sampson Low, 1932.

McGowan, Norman. *My Years With Churchill.* London: Pan Books, 1959.

Menzies, Robert. *Afternoon Light: Some Memories of Men and Events.* London: Cassell, 1967.

Montgomery, Bernard. *Memoirs of Field Marshal Montgomery.* London: Collins, 1968.

Moran, Lord. *Churchill: Taken from the Diaries of Lord Moran. The Struggle for Survival 1940–1965.* Boston: Houghton Mifflin, 1966.

Morgan, Ted. *Churchill: The Rise to Failure 1874–1915.* London: Jonathan Cape, 1983.

Murray, Edmund. *I Was Churchill's Bodyguard.* London: W.H. Allen, 1987.

Nel, Elizabeth. *Mr Churchill's Secretary.* London: Hodder & Stoughton, 1958.

Nemon, Oscar. Unpublished memoirs, by courtesy of Lady Young and James R. Lancaster, 2007.

Nicolson, Nigel, ed. *Harold Nicolson: Diaries and Letters.* 3 vols. London: Collins, 1966–68.

Nicolson, Nigel, ed. *The Harold Nicolson Diaries 1907–1963.* London: Weidenfeld & Nicolson, 2004.

Pawle, Gerald. *The War and Colonel Warden.* London: George G. Harrap & Co., 1963.

Pelling, Henry. *Winston Churchill.* Revised and extended softbound edition. Ware, Herts.: Wordsworth Editions, 1999.

Pilpel, Robert. *Churchill in America 1895–1961.* New York: Harcourt, Brace, Jovanovich, 1976.

Pottle, Mark, ed. *Champion Redoubtable: The Diaries and Letters of Violet Bonham Carter 1914–45.* London: Weidenfeld & Nicolson, 1998.

Reynolds, David. *In Command of History: Churchill Writing and Fighting the Second World War.* London: Allen Lane, 2004.

Reynolds, Quentin. *All About Winston Churchill.* London: W. H. Allen, 1964.

Roberts, Andrew. *Eminent Churchillians.* London: Weidenfeld & Nicolson, 1994.

Rose, Norman. *Churchill: An Unruly Life.* London: Simon & Schuster, 1994.

Rowse, A.L. *The Later Churchills.* London: Macmillan, 1958.

Salter, Kay and Jim. *Life is Meals: A Food Lover's Book of Days*. New York: Knopf, 2006.

Sandys, Celia. *From Winston with Love and Kisses*. London: Sinclair Stevenson, 1994.

Shapiro, Fred, ed. *Yale Book of Quotations*. New Haven, Ct.: Yale University Press, 2007.

Sherwood, Robert. *The White House Papers of Harry L. Hopkins*. (2 vols.) London: Eyre & Spottiswoode, 1948.

Soames, Mary. *Clementine Churchill*. London: Cassell, 1979.

_____, ed. *Speaking for Themselves: The Personal Letters of Winston and Clementine Churchill*. London: Doubleday, 1998.

Sykes, Christopher. *Nancy Astor*. New York: Harper & Row, 1972.

Taylor, Robert Louis. *Winston Churchill: An Informal Study of Greatness*. Garden City, N.Y.: Doubleday, 1952.

Tedder, Arthur (Lord). *With Prejudice: The War Memoirs of Marshal of the Royal Airforce Lord Tedder*. London: Cassell, 1966.

Thompson, R.W. *The Yankee Marlborough*. London: George Allen & Unwin, 1963.

Thompson, Walter H. *I Was Churchill's Shadow*. London: Christopher Johnson, 1951.

Thompson, W.H., *Assignment Churchill*. New York: Farar, Straus & Young, 1955.

Thornton-Kemsley, Colin. *Through Winds and Tides*. Montrose: Standard Press, 1974.

Ward, Geoffrey C., ed. *Closest Companion: The Unknown Story of the Intimate Friendship between Franklin Roosevelt and Margaret Suckley*. New York: Houghton Mifflin, 1995.

Wheeler-Bennett, John, ed. *Action This Day: Working with Churchill*. London: Macmillan, 1968.

Young. *Churchill and Beaverbrook*. London: Eyre & Spottiswood, 1966.

Interviews

Peregrine Spencer Churchill, WSC's nephew; Clark Clifford, aide to President Truman; Ronald Golding, bodyguard 1946–7; Grace Hamblin, secretary 1932–65; Sir John Colville, private secretary 1940–1, 1943–5, principal private secretary 1951–5; Sir Fitzroy Maclean, British mission to Tito 1943–5; Sir Anthony Montague Browne, personal private secretary 1952–65; Edmund Murray, bodyguard 1950–65; Christian Pol-Roger; Lord and Lady Soames.

Bibliographical notes

1. Thrusts and parries

Aborigine missionaries 1 May

Above comprehension *1*. 18 November; *2*. 19 November

Abstaining 13 December

Abuse 26 February

Agitated opponents 15 December

Alcohol *1*. Chartwell (Sir Anthony Montague Browne to the Churchill Centre, London, 1985); *2*. passim

Anglo-American mongrel Cawthorne 1965, 32

Baskets in egg October (Lord Boyd of Merson to the Edmonton Churchill Society, 1973)

Baths 28 October

Bloody black sheep 29 October

Brighton *1*. Lord Boyd to David Dilks; *2*. Macmillan 1969, 488

Bring a friend London (Dalton Newfield)

Combing out 23 May

Constipation Lord Carrington (*Finest Hour*, summer *2001, 19*)

Crackling of thorns 28 October

Craft 11 November

Crooked deal Halle 1966, 112

Damned old fool 19 April

de Gaulle, Charles *1*. Halle 1966, 213; *2*. 2 April (Dilks, Winter–Spring 1975)

Dead birds Buckingham Palace (Ronald Golding to the editor)

Dead or alive January ('The Irish Treaty', *Pall Mall*; *Thoughts and Adventures* 1932, 161–2)

Deaf member Cawthorne 1965, 24–5

Discards Bonham Carter 1965, 279

Doing what is right Harold Macmillan to David Dilks

Driving on the left June, Hyde Park (Halle 1970, 32)

Drunk and ugly Ronald Golding to the editor

Facts 9 February

Fair case Macmillan 1969, 391

Feet on the ground 28 October

Food Ministry 27 October

Foot and mouth disease 6 May

Force and favour Sir John Foster, MP, in Halle 1966, 331

Foreign secretaries unite 7 May (Colville 1976, 242–3)

Foresight 23 July

Frustrated teacher 1 December (Nicolson 1907–63, 394)

God and the House Chequers (Bill Deakin to David Dilks)

Guillotine 29 April (Halle 1966, 115)

Guilty conscience 17 November (*Blood, Sweat and Tears* 1941, 106)

Gut meets gut L. Burgis to Randolph Churchill, 1963; Burgis Papers 1/3, Churchill College

Hanging *1*. 15 July; *2*. 17 January, Press conference, Washington (McGowan 1959, 222)

Health 30 November, Hyde Park Gate, London (McGowan 1959; Manchester 1983, 34)

Impartial historian 26 April

Indians 5 September, White House, Washington (Pawle 1963, 250; Pilpel 1976, 199; Ward 1995, 235)

Indignation *1*. 23 February; *2*. 6 December

Ingratitude Halle 1966, 131

Jujube 15 February (Channon 1967, 453–4)

Korea vs Crimea 28 May

Korean armaments 28 May

2. Maxims and reflections

News making *The Story of the Malakand Field Force 1897* 1991, 97

Old and new 6 January (*The Second World War* 1948–54, III, 638)

Opportunity 29 January

Parliament 6 June

Peacekeeping 14 April

Perfection *1.* 6 December (*The Second World War* 1948–54, IV, 808); *2.* 17 November, Sheffield

Perseverance *1.* January; *2.* Nel 1958, 37; *3.* 26 March (*The Second World War* 1948–54, III, 142); *4.* 29 October, Harrow School (*The Unrelenting Struggle* 1942, 286); *5.* 29 October, Harrow School (*The Unrelenting Struggle* 1942, 287)

Personal relations 24 May

Personnel 17 February (Kennedy 1957, 80)

Pleasure 6 November

Political action 26 July, North-west Manchester (*Winston S. Churchill: His Complete Speeches 1897–1963*, 1974, I, 413)

Politicians July ('Alfonso the Unlucky', *Strand Magazine*; *Great Contemporaries*, 131)

Politics 16 August, Aldershot (Official Biography, CV1/1, 583)

Power *1.* 28 February; *2.* 3 March; *3.* 28 April; *4.* 14 January, Château Laurier, Ottawa (*Stemming the Tide* 1953, 218)

Principles *1.* 31 March, London (*The Second World War* 1948–54, I, 164); *2.* 29 November, Cairo (*The Second World War* 1948–54, V, 637); *3.* 17 March party political broadcast, London (*Stemming the Tide* 1953, 34)

Prophets 30 April

Quarrels 10 August ('The Spanish Tragedy', *Evening Standard*; *Step by Step* 1936, 38)

Recrimination *1.* 29 May; *2.* 14 March; *3.* 18 June

Redress of grievances November ('The Truth about Hitler', *Strand Magazine*; *Great Contemporaries*, 167)

Repetition *The Second World War* 1948–54, I, 374

Resources 2 February (Official Biography, CV2/3, 1861)

Retrospect *1.* 16 April; *2.* 2 March, Royal College of Physicians, London (*The Dawn of Liberation* 1945, 24)

Right and consistent 11 October (*Stemming the Tide* 1953, 344)

Right and hard 9 October, Llandudno, Wales (*Europe Unite* 1950, 419)

Right and honest 16 November, Free Trade Hall, Manchester (*Winston S. Churchill: His Complete Speeches 1897–1963*, 1974, IV, 3399)

Right and irresponsible 26 August, party political broadcast, London (*In the Balance: Speeches 1949 & 1950* 1951, 355)

Right and wrong 27 May (*The Second World War* 1948–54, VI, 504)

Risk 19 February, Cingolo Neck, South Africa (*London to Ladysmith via Pretoria* 1900, 388–9; *The Boer War* 1989, 175)

Safety *The Second World War* 1948–54, IV, 14

Satisfaction 26 December (*The Second World War* 1948–54, V, 385)

Secrets 31 March, near Pieters, Natal, South Africa (*Ian Hamilton's March* 1900, 4; *The Boer War* 1989, 226)

Settlements *1.* 27 January, Treasury, London (*Winston S. Churchill: His Complete Speeches 1897–1963*, 1974, IV, 3824); *2.* 16 February

Shot at without result *The Story of the Malakand Field Force 1897* 1989, 117

Simplicity *1.* *The World Crisis* 1923–31, III, Part 1, 140; *2.* 27 March; *3.* 14 May, United Europe meeting, Albert Hall, London (*Europe Unite* 1950, 77)

Social reform 4 October, Brighton (*Europe Unite* 1950, 158)

Solvency 5 March

Speechmaking March (Ben-Moshe 1992, 282)

Spite 26 May (*The Second World War* 1948–54, V, 628)

Success 13 December (*The Second World War* 1948–54, II, 541)

Sufficiency 25 April

Temptations *Savrola* 1990 edn, 114

Theory and practice 19 March (Diaries of cabinet secretary Sir Norman Brook, *New York Times*, 22 January 2006)

Thought *1. My Early Life* 1930, 127; 2. 19 July (*The Second World War* 1948–54, II, 21); 3. *The Second World War* 1948–54, V, 514

Thrift 10 October, Dundee (*The People's Rights* 1990, 146)

Tidiness and symmetry 22 October

Time *1.* 19 July; 2. 30 April, Albert Hall, London (*Europe Unite*, 308)

Tributes 29 April

Trust 13 April, Bethany, South Africa (*Ian Hamilton's March* 1900, 24; *The Boer War* 1989, 235)

Truth *1.* 17 May; 2. 8 May (Official Biography, CV6 /1, 1247); 3. 30 November, Teheran (*The Second World War* 1948–54, V, 338); 4. 14 February, Athens (*Victory* 1946, 42); 5. 28 March

Tyranny 15 November, Brussels University (*The Sinews of Peace: Post-War Speeches* 1948, 38)

Unexpected 7 May, London (*The Sinews of Peace: Post-War Speeches* 1948, 123)

Unteachable mankind 21 May, Exchequer (Official Biography, CV5/1, 1291)

Vanquished enemies 5 February, Yalta (Gilbert 1991, 818)

Vengeance *1.* 5 June; 2. 10 December

Virtue vs wickedness *The Second World War* 1948–54, I, 149

Virtuous circle 24 April, broadcast, London (*Winston S. Churchill: His Complete Speeches 1897–1963*, 1974, IV, 4400)

War and democracy (Official Biography, VIII, 369)

War and peace *My Early Life* 1930, 346

War wounds South Africa (Taylor 1952, 173)

Weakness and treason *The Second World War* 1948–54, I, 154

Wealth and commonwealth *1.* 29 December ('Roosevelt from Afar', *Colliers; Great Contemporaries* 1990, 241); 2. 16 August; 3. 12 March

Wicked and dictators *The Second World War* 1948–54, III, 329

Win or lose 25 June

Wisdom *1.* 5 October; 2. 10 September

Women *Savrola* 1990 edn, 57

Work *1.* December ('Hobbies', *Pall Mall; Thoughts and Adventures* 1932, 217); 2. August ('Herbert Henry Asquith', *Pall Mall; Great Contemporaries*, 86)

World War II: 1940 *The Second World War* 1948–54, II, 555

World War II: Moral *My Early Life* 1930, 346

Wrongdoing 22 February

Youth 29 November (*The Dawn of Liberation* 1945, 260)

3. Stories and jokes

Bear, buffalo and donkey 1 August (Pelling 1999, 546; Wheeler-Bennett 1968, 96)

Disarmament fable 25 October, Aldersbrook Road, West Essex (then part of his constituency) (*Arms and the Covenant* 1938, 17)

4. Churchillisms

Terminological inexactitude 22 February (Official Biography, II, 167)

Thirteen feet of minister Alan Lennox-Boyd, later Lord Boyd, to David Dilks

Toil, blood, death, squalor 10 March, radio interview, New York (Gilbert 1982, 45)

Triphibian 31 August, broadcast, London (*Onwards to Victory* 1944, 179)

Ungrateful volcano 1 September (Official Biography, CV4/3, 1974)

Unregulated unthinkability 14 March

Unsordid 17 April

Wincing marquess 26 July, St Andrew's Hall, Norwich (*Winston S. Churchill: His Complete Speeches 1897–1963*, 1974, II, 1294)

Winstonian 9 May, Mount Street, London (Official Biography, CV2/1, 391)

Woomany 12 January (Official Biography, CV 1/1, 152)

Wormwood Scrubbery 12 March

Wounded canary 2 April (Nicolson II, 358)

Wuthering Height 'Churchill the Conversationalist', by Colin Brooks, in Eade 1953, 246

5. Great communicator

Book composition Graebner 1965, 69

Books: his own *1*. 17 February, Authors' Club, London (*Winston S. Churchill: His Complete Speeches 1897–1963*, 1974, I, 903); 2. Tedder 1966, Preface; *3*. 2 November, Grosvenor House, London (Churchill Archives Centre); *4*. 4 July, Royal United Services Institution, London (*In the Balance: Speeches 1949 & 1950* 1951, 304)

Breadth of a comma 7 July

Brevity *1*. Gretton 1968, passim; *2*. 27 January (*The Second World War* 1948–54, IV, 752); *3*. 24 June, Marshall's Manor, Sussex (Moran 1966, 746)

Chartwell factory Hamblin 1989

Classical literature *My Early Life* 1930, 37

'Consultation' 7 May

Curate's egg 21 April, Royal Albert Hall, London (*Europe Unite* 1950, 301)

Dictation *1*. Lord Boyd of Merton to David Dilks; *2*. Hamblin 1989

Drafts *1*. 14 May (Official Biography, VIII, 331); *2. (*Official Biography, VIII, 528)

English 8 August, English-Speaking Union Dinner, London (*The Unwritten Alliance* 1961, 154)

Facts vs rumour *Marlborough: His Life and Times* 1933–8, I, 300

Foreign names and pronunciation *1*. 18 December; *2*. 'Churchill the Conversationalist', by Collin Brooks, in Eade 1953, 247; *3*. Pawle 1963, 68; *4*. 7 May; *5*. Nicolson 2004, 269; *6*. 13 February, Yalta (Halle 1966, 160); *7*. 23 April (*The Second World War* 1948–54, VI, 642–3)

'Grand Remonstrance' *My Early Life* 1930, 125

History 12 November

Hyphens and 'e's' 22 June (CV5/1 814–5)

Jargon *The Second World War* 1948–54, IV, 516

Language *1*. 9 December; *2*. 15 July

Latin *1*. *My Early Life* 1930, 37; *2*. 5 March

Leave the past to history 23 January

Maiden speech *1*. 18 February; *2*. *My Early Life* 1930, 378–80

Man vs woman 8 December (*Winston S. Churchill: His Complete Speeches 1897–1963*, 1974, VII, 7051)

Mein Kampf as a Koran *The Second World War* 1948–54, I, 43

Melting 2 March (Official Biography, CV5/2, 1097)

6. People

Bossom, Alfred Lord Mountbatten to the Edmonton Churchill Society, 1966

Bryan, William Jennings 31 August (Official Biography, CV1 PART 1, 678)

Buller, Redvers *My Early Life* 1930, 248

Butler, R. A. 1 December

Cecil, Lord Hugh February ('Personal Contacts', *Strand Magazine*; *Thoughts and Adventures* 1932, 35)

Chamberlain, Austen *1.* 18 May, Edinburgh (Morgan 1983, 191); *2.* 13 February, Yalta (Moran 1966, 253)

Chamberlain, Joseph *1.* April (Taylor 1952, quoting Herbert Vivian in *Pall Mall*); *2.* 29 January, Nottingham (*Winston S. Churchill: His Complete Speeches 1897–1963*, 1974, II, 1105)

Chamberlain, Neville *1.* February (Broad 1945, 255); *2.* Drumlanraig, Scotland (Gilbert 1994, 23); *3.* 12 November; *4.* 22 November (Nicolson II, 129)

Chaplin, Charlie 29 September, Barstow, California (Official Biography, CV5/2, 97)

Churchill, Lady Randolph 29 July (Official Biography, CV4/3, 1525)

Churchill, Winston (American novelist) *1.* 7 June, London (*My Early Life* 1930, 231–2); *2.* 17 December, Boston (Official Biography, I, 353)

Cripps, Stafford *1.* December (Colville 1986–7, vol. I, 368); *2.* 19 May, Washington ('Churchill the Conversationalist', by Colin Brooks, in Eade 1953, 247); *3.* 12 December

Cromwell, Oliver *My Early Life* 1930, 16

Crossman, R. H. S. 14 July

Curzon, George January ('George Curzon', *Pall Mall*; *Great Contemporaries*, 174, 184)

Dalton, Hugh *1.* 10 May; *2.* 14 February, broadcast, London (*Europe Unite*, 242)

de Gaulle, Charles *1.* 10 January, Casablanca (Halle 1966, 212); *2.* May, Ottawa (Birkenhead 1966, 537)

de Valera, Eamon *1.* 4 February ('The Dusk of the League', *Daily Telegraph; Step by Step* 1938, 198); *2.* 5 May

Dulles, John Foster *1.* 7 January (Colville 1986–7, II, 320); *2.* Anthony Montague Browne to the Churchill Centre, London, 1985; *3.* 7 December, Bermuda (Moran 1966, 540–1); *4.* Macmillan 1969, 489; *5.* 24 June, Washington (Halle 1966, 325)

Halifax, Earl Viscount De L'Isle VC to the Edmonton Churchill Society, 1985

Hearst, William Randolph 29 September, Barstow, California (Official Biography, CV5/2, 96)

Hitler, Adolf *1.* 4 October (*The Second World War* 1948–54, II, 441); *2.* 10 May, broadcast, London (*The End of the Beginning* 1943, 126); *3.* 28 September; *4.* 28 September

Hopkins, Harry 15 January, Casablanca (Soames 1998, 473)

Inönü, Ismet 7 December, Constantinople (Eden 1965, 429)

Joynson-Hicks, William 9 August (*Sunday Pictorial*, 8)

King Edward VII 22 January, Winnipeg, Manitoba (Official Biography, CV1 part 2, 1231)

King Ibn Saud 17 February, Lake Fayyum, Egypt (Gilbert 1991, 825)

Kinna, Patrick English Channel (Kinna family to Paul H. Courtenay)

Kitchener, Field Marshal Lord *The World Crisis* 1923–31, I, 234

Lenin,Vladimir *1.* 5 November; *2.* *The World Crisis* 1923–31, IV, 74–6

7. Britain, Empire and Commonwealth

Gibraltar 1 September (*The Second World War* 1948–54, VI, 607)

Humbug *My Early Life* 1930, 70

London *1.* 9 May, Ministry of Health, London; *2.* 9 November, Lord Mayor's Banquet, Guildhall, London (*The Unwritten Alliance* 1961, 192)

Obligations 22 December, broadcast, London (*Stemming the Tide* 1953, 214)

People *1.* 13 May; *2.* 13 April; *3.* Ronald Golding to the editor

People in war *1.* 11 September, London Opera House (Official Biography, III, 76); *2.* 9 November, Guildhall, London (*Winston S. Churchill: His Complete Speeches 1897–1963*, 1974, III, 2340); *3.* 2 April (*The Second World War* 1948–54, VI, 431)

Scotland *1.* 3 January, Belgium (Official Biography, CV3/2, 1354); *2.* 12 October, Usher Hall, Edinburgh (*The End of the Beginning* 1943, 237)

Uganda *1.* Editor's Observation; *2.* *My African Journey*, 103

Virgin Islands Downing Street. (Sir Alexander Cadogan to David Dilks)

Wales 6 November

8. Nations

Australia *A History of the English-Speaking Peoples* 1956–8, IV, 122

Canada *1.* 22 January, Winnipeg, Manitoba (Official Biography, CV1/2, 1231); *2.* 19 July; *3.* 4 September, Mansion House, London (*The Unrelenting Struggle* 1942, 244); *4.* 31 December, Press conference, Ottawa (Dilks, 2005, 220); *5.* 30 June, broadcast, Ottawa (Dilks, 2005, 426)

China *1.* 3 September ('The Wounded Dragon', *Evening Standard*; *Step by Step* 1937, 151, 153); *2.* 17 January, Congress, Washington (*Stemming the Tide* 1953, 223)

Cuba 15 December, New York (Official Biography, CV1/1, 620)

Czechoslovakia 16 October, London, broadcast to the United States (*Blood, Sweat and Tears* 1941, 84)

Denmark 10 October, Copenhagen University. (*In the Balance: Speeches 1949 & 1950* 1951, 387)

Egypt *1.* *The River War* 1899, I, 152–3; *2.* 3 April, Cairo (Official Biography, I, 441); *3.* *The Second World War* 1948–54, V, 371

France *1.* 25 June ('Vive La France!', *Evening Standard*; *Step by Step* 19XX, 131–2); *2.* 21 October, London, broadcast to France (*Blood, Sweat and Tears* 1941, 463; *Winston S. Churchill: His Complete Speeches 1897–1963*, 1974, VI, 6297); *3.* 10 December; *4.* 12 November, Hotel de Ville, Paris. (*The Dawn of Liberation* 1945, 246)

Germany *1.* 13 July; *2.* Lord Mountbatten to the Edmonton Churchill Society, 1966; *3.* 19 May, Congress, Washington (*Onwards to Victory* 1944, 100)

Greece *1.* 7 May; *2.* *The Second World War* 1948–54, V, 470–1

India *1.* *The Story of the Malakand Field Force 1897* 1989, 193; *2.* 26 March, Constitutional Club, London (*Winston S. Churchill: His Complete Speeches 1897–1963*, 1974, V, 5011)

Ireland *1.* 8 May; *2.* 15 December; *3.* 16 February; *4.* 12 April; *5.* *My Early Life* 1930, 16; *6.* 'The Dream', (Official Biography, VIII, 368)

Israel 18 February (Official Biography, VIII, 1095)

Italy *1.* 16 February, Ditchley Park (Kennedy 1957, 79); *2.* 29 November, London, world broadcast (*The End of the Beginning* 1943, 299)

Japan *1.* 8 December, London (*The Second World War* 1948–54, III,

542–3); *2*. 26 December, Congress, Washington (*The Unrelenting Struggle* 1942, 359–60)

Jordan 24 March

Morocco *1. The Second World War* 1948–54, IV, 622; *2*. 25 December, Marrakesh (Soames 1998, 558)

Palestine 1 August

Poland 7 February, Yalta (Official Biography, VII, 1189)

Russia *1*. 24 January, Paris. (Gilbert 1991, 408); *2*. 8 April, Paris (Official Biography, CV4/1, 609); *3*. 5 November; *4*. July ('Mass Effects in Modern Life', *Pall Mall*; *Thoughts and Adventures* 1932, 185); *5. The World Crisis* 1923–31, IV, 235; *6. The World Crisis* 1923–31, V, 350; *7*. 1 October, broadcast, London (*Blood, Sweat and Tears* 1941, 205–6); *8*. 23 April; *9*. The Dream (Official Biography, VIII, 371; *10*. 26 January)

South Africa 18 February

Spain July ('Alfonso XIII', *Strand Magazine*; *Great Contemporaries*, 137)

Sudan *1. The River War* 1899, I, 156; *2. The River War* 1899, I, 290; *3. The River War* 1899, II, 162

United States of America *1*. 10 November, New York (Official Biography, I, CV1/1, 597); *2*. 12 November, New York. (Official Biography, CV1/1, 598); *3*. 15 November, New York (Official Biography, CV1/1, 600); *4*. 8 December, Press Club, New York (Pilpel, 1976, 36); *5*. 7 July (Official Biography, CV5/2, 16); *6*. February ('Personal Contacts', *Strand Magazine*; *Thoughts and Adventures* 1932, 32); *7*. 14 August ('Prohibition', *The Sunday Chronicle*; *Collected Essays* 1975, IV, 111); *8*. 5 August ('Land of Corn and Lobsters', *Collier's*; *Collected Essays* 1975, IV, 263); *9*. 8 October

(Halle 1966, 7–8); *10*. 20 August (Official Biography, VI, 743); *11*. 10 November, Mansion House, London (*The Unrelenting Struggle* 1942, 298); *12*. 9 December (Bryant, 1957, 231); *13*. 26 December, Congress, Washington (*The Unrelenting Struggle* 1942, 353–4); *14*. August, Niagara Falls (Official Biography, VII, 469); *15*. August, Press conference, Quebec (Graebner 1965, 106); *16*. September, Press conference, Washington. (Halle 1966, 240); *17*. 4 March, en route to Fulton, Missouri (Halle 1970, 17); *18*. Ibid., 34–5; *19*. Graebner 1965, 106; *20*. 1 April, Boston (Reynolds 2004, 201; *21. The Second World War* 1948–54, V, 494; *22*. 16 January, Washington (*Winston S. Churchill: His Complete Speeches 1897–1963*, 1974, VIII, 8323); *23*. 27 March, St Stephen's Hall, London. (*The Unwritten Alliance* 1961, 26); *24*. Downing Street. (Nemon, 51B); *25*. 28 June, Press conference, Washington. (Pilpel 1976, 262)

Yugoslavia December (Maclean, Churchill Proceedings, 1987)

9. War

Admirals December (*The Second World War* 1948–54, III, 591–2)

Air Power *1*. 28 November; *2*. 20 June; *3*. 6 September, Harvard University, Cambridge, Massachusetts (*Onwards to Victory* 1944, 182)

Allies 10 December (*Secret Session Speeches* 1946, 79)

Army 8 August

Artillery 23 April, St George's Day dinner, Honourable Artillery Company (*The Unwritten Alliance* 1961, 36)

Bedding down 1. *My Early Life* 1930, 99; 2. *My Early Life* 1930, 332

Boer War 1. 15 November, Chieveley, South Africa (Maccallum Scott, 43); 2. 10 December, Pretoria (*London to Ladysmith via Pretoria*, 1900, 176–7; *The Boer War* 1989, 78–9); 3. 22 December, South Africa (*London to Ladysmith via Pretoria* 1900, 195–6; *The Boer War* 1989, 87)

Cavalry *My Early Life* 1930, 78

Death by bombing 21 November (Cadogan, 682)

Democracy in wartime England (Pottle, 247)

Deterrence 24 March

Enemy, handling the 1. *My Early Life* 1930, 346; 2. 23 September (Official Biography, VI, 803)

Generals 1. 23 February (MBA, 92); 2. 1 March (Gilbert 1991, 170)

Infantry Ismay 1960, 270

Military branches 1. 16 November (Macmillan, Blast, 352); 2. *The Second World War* 1948–54, IV, 584

Navy, American 9 May (*The Second World War* 1948–54, IV, 273)

Nuclear Deterrent 14 December

Officers 1. Maclean, Churchill Proceedings, 1987; 2. 27 January, Ploegsteert, Belgium (Official Biography, III, 651)

Reflections on War 1. 22 February, Flanders. (Soames 1998, 179); 2. *My Early Life* 1930, 79; 3. The Dream (Official Biography, VIII, 371); 4. 31 March, Massachusetts Institute Of Technology, Boston (*In the Balance: Speeches 1949 & 1950* 1951, 40–2)

Royal Naval College 1. May, RNC, Devonport (Lord Mountbatten to the Edmonton Churchill Society, 1966); 2. Menzies 1967, 74

Sea battle 1. 18 March; 2. 17 March

Submarine hunting 1. March (*The World Crisis* 1923–31, III, Part 2, 366); 2. *The Sunday Times*, 13 July 1980

Tanks 1. 2 July; 2. 23 April (*The Second World War* 1948–54, IV, 850)

Under fire 1. 15 November, Chieveley, South Africa (Taylor 1952, 173); 2. *London to Ladysmith via Pretoria* 1900, 137; *The Boer War* 1989, 61

World War I 1. 15 November; 2. Cowles 1953, 210; 3. 3 January, Flanders (Official Biography, CV3/2, 1354); 4. 24 March (*The World Crisis* 1923–31, III, Part 2, 423); 5. *The World Crisis* 1923–31, I, 11; 6. 27 March

World War II prelude 1. 14 March; 2. 30 July; 3. May, Moscow, published 1948 (*The Second World War* 1948–54, I, 105–6); 4. 8 January, Marrakesh (Official Biography, CV5/3, 10); 5. 12 November; 6. March (Guedalla, 271–2); 7. 1 March (Nicolson I, 328); 8. 11 September, Chartwell (CV5/3, 1155); 9. 8 August, London, broadcast to United States (*Blood, Sweat and Tears* 1941, 196–7)

World War II 1. 3 September, published 1948 (*The Second World War* 1948–54, I, 319); 2. 26 June (Official Biography, CV6/1, 148); 3. 1 October, broadcast, London (*Blood, Sweat and Tears* 1941, 206); 4. 30 March, broadcast, London (*Blood, Sweat and Tears* 1941, 290); 5. June, published 1948 (*The Second World War* 1948–54, II, 404); 6. 5 September; 7. 31 August, Chequers (Official Biography, CV6/2, 749); 8. September, published 1948 (*The Second World War* 1948–54, II, 320); 9. 12 December, published 1949 (*The Second World War* 1948–54, II, 547); 10. 22 January; 11. 22 January; 12. 15 March; 13. 8 April (*The Second World War* 1948–54, IV, 640); 14. 30 May (*The Second World War* 1948–54, V, 66); 15. 21 June, Chequers (Colville 1986–7, I,

10. Politics and Government

Bangalore, India (Official Biography, CV1/2, 938)

Political parties 25 June

Politicians *1. Morning Post* interview; Halle 1966, 49; *2.* 17 November, Institute of Journalists dinner, London (*Winston S. Churchill: His Complete Speeches 1897–1963*, 1974, I, 693)

Polls 30 September

Poverty 4 January, Manchester (Marsh 1939, 150)

Prime Minister 24 July

Private enterprise 29 September, Woodford, Essex (*The Unwritten Alliance* 1961, 324)

Revolution 10 October

Socialists *1.* 11 October, St. Andrew's Hall, Glasgow ('Liberalism and the Social Problem', reprinted in *The Collected Works*, Vol. VII, Early Speeches, 160); *2.* 14 February (*Sunday Express*); *3.* 23 July, Wolverhampton (*Winston S. Churchill: His Complete Speeches 1897–1963*, 1974, VII, 7831–2)

Summit conferences 16 September, Quebec (*The Dawn of Liberation* 1945, 173)

Taxation *1.* 12 May; *2.* 1 June (Taylor 1952, 222)

Vote of Confidence *1.* 6 April; *2.* 29 January (Moran 1966, 27)

Warmongering 17 March

War Office *1.* June (Moran 1966, 36); *2.* 2 August

Wisdom and Folly 10 September, Guildhall, London (*Europe Unite* 1950, 138–9)

Women in politics 'The Dream' (Official Biography, VIII, 368)

11. Education, Arts and Science

Arts *1.* 1 June (Official Biography, VI, 449); *2. Savrola* 1990 edn, 75

Cancer 19 June

Classics *1.* 10 July (Moran 1966, 281); *2.* 12 May, University Of Oslo (*Europe Unite* 1950, 326)

Disease *The Second World War* 1948– 54, II, 317

English *My Early Life* 1930, 31

Explosives Admiralty, London (Halle 1966, 171)

Guided missiles 15 March (Official Biography, VIII, 714)

Latin *My Early Life* 1930, 36

Metaphysics *My Early Life* 1930, 131–2

Public Schools *1. My Early Life* 1930, 53; *2.* 18 December, Harrow School (*The Unrelenting Struggle* 1942, 20)

RMS *Queen Mary* May ('Queen of the Seas', *Strand Magazine*; *Collected Essays* 1975, IV, 332)

Socrates *My Early Life* 1930, 124

Technology 18 November, University Of London (*Europe Unite* 1950, 468)

Television *1.* Press conference, New York (Halle 1966, 307); *2.* London. Editor's Observation

12. Personal

Advice 27 June (Amery, J., 270)

Afterlife *1.* Graebner 1965, 24–5); *2.* Clark Clifford to the editor; *3.* 21 January (Moran 1966, 556)

Aging Halle 1966, 337

Alcohol *1.* passim ('Churchill the Conversationalist', by Colin Brooks, in Eade 1953, 248); *2. My Early Life* 1930, 141; *3.* Menzies 1967, 93; *4.* January (A. P. Herbert in Halle 1966, 187); *5.* 21 January, Casablanca (Sherwood II, 682); *6.* 22 January, Casablanca (Sherwood, II, 685); *7.* 27 October (Cadogan, 675); *8.* 8 December (*The Dawn of Liberation* 1945, 281); *9.* Epernay Christian Pol-Roger to the editor; *10.* 17 January, Washington (Halle 1966, 268);

Biography, CV2/2, 914); *2.* 5 August ('Land of Corn and Lobsters', Collier's; *Collected Essays* 1975, IV, 262); *3.* Downing Street ('Churchill the Conversationalist', by Colin Brooks, in Eade 1953, 363); *4.* 14 July (Colville 1976, 98); *5.* Chequers (Pawle 1963, 172); *6.* August en route from Teheran to Moscow (Pawle 1963, 5); *7.* Graebner 1965, 61; *8.* Macmillan, Winds, 29

Painting *1.* December ('Painting as a Pastime', *Strand Magazine*; *Thoughts and Adventures* 1932, 223–4); *2.* December ('Painting as a Pastime', *Strand Magazine*; *Thoughts and Adventures* 1932, 224–5); *3.* January ('Painting as a Pastime', *Strand Magazine*; *Thoughts and Adventures* 1932, 229–30); *4.* Peregrine Churchill to the editor; *5.* Sandys, 141; *6.* Churchill, J., 100–1; *7.* Ronald Golding to the editor

Predestination 18 September (Barnes & Nicholson, 642)

Prodding 11 November

Prophesying 1 February (Press conference, Cairo; *Onwards to Victory* 1944, 7)

Religion *1.* Dalton, *New Statesman*, 1965; *2.* On the Atlantic (Gilbert 1994, 227); *3. My Early Life* 1930, 127–8; *4.* 25 December, Washington (Moran 1966, 14); *5.* Chartwell (Graebner 1965, 25); *6.* Official Biography, VIII, 1161

Retirement *1.* Cowles 1953, 356; *2.* Macdonald, 124; *3.* 8 February, New York (*Sunday Times,* London); *4.* 12 March (Official Biography, VIII, 958)

Reward poster Taylor 1952, 186

Rudeness Howells, 61

Running 4 February (*The Second World War* 1948–54, III, 647)

Self-expression *1.* Bonham Carter 1965, 16; *2. My Early Life* 1930, 118; *3.* 8 August, Chequers (Moran 1966, 478)

Servants Golfe Juan, France (Sir John Colville to the editor)

Sex *1.* Graebner 1965, 25; *2.* 7 April

Skin Bonham Carter 1965, 230

Staphylococcus 27 June (Moran 1966, 335–6)

Suicide Macmillan 1969, 489

Thought Home, Wind, 84

Trinity *1.* 10 September, Antwerp (Halle 1966, 75); *2.* Colville 1976, 258

Unpunctuality *My Early Life* 1930, 107

Volubility 20 January (Gilbert 1991, 633)

Writing *The Second World War* 1948– 54, I, 62

Appendix

Beer bottles 4 June BBC (Taylor 1952, 223–4)

Cigars and women July, August (*American Spectator*)

Democracy *1.* 11 November (*Europe Unite* 1950, 200)

Dinner, wine and women Salter, 409.

Dukes 9 October, Newcastle

Golf Manchester 1983, 213

Ingratitude *The Second World War* 1948–54, I, 10

Jaw, jaw Washington (*Finest Hour* 122, 15)

Lies 22 February

Monarchy constitutional 15 May

Naval tradition Admiralty

Poison in your coffee Blenheim Palace (Balsan, 162; Sykes, 127)

Prepositions 27 February (Benjamin Zimmer, http://xrl.us/izbq)

Simple tastes passim

Virtues and vices Adler, 29

Index of names

Index

PublicAffairs is a publishing house founded in 1997. It is a tribute to the standards, values, and flair of three persons who have served as mentors to countless reporters, writers, editors, and book people of all kinds, including me.

I. F. STONE, proprietor of *I. F. Stone's Weekly*, combined a commitment to the First Amendment with entrepreneurial zeal and reporting skill and became one of the great independent journalists in American history. At the age of eighty, Izzy published *The Trial of Socrates*, which was a national bestseller. He wrote the book after he taught himself ancient Greek.

BENJAMIN C. BRADLEE was for nearly thirty years the charismatic editorial leader of *The Washington Post*. It was Ben who gave the *Post* the range and courage to pursue such historic issues as Watergate. He supported his reporters with a tenacity that made them fearless and it is no accident that so many became authors of influential, best-selling books.

ROBERT L. BERNSTEIN, the chief executive of Random House for more than a quarter century, guided one of the nation's premier publishing houses. Bob was personally responsible for many books of political dissent and argument that challenged tyranny around the globe. He is also the founder and longtime chair of Human Rights Watch, one of the most respected human rights organizations in the world.

     •   •   •

For fifty years, the banner of Public Affairs Press was carried by its owner Morris B. Schnapper, who published Gandhi, Nasser, Toynbee, Truman, and about 1,500 other authors. In 1983, Schnapper was described by *The Washington Post* as "a redoubtable gadfly." His legacy will endure in the books to come.

Peter Osnos, *Founder and Editor-at-Large*